input

CUP04/52
£13

RA

14

cookbynumbers™
indian

Mahboob Momen

cookbynumbers™

...real cooking made easy

indian

CASSELL ILLUSTRATED

First published in Great Britain in 2004 by Cassell Illustrated,
a division of Octopus Publishing Group Limited
2–4 Heron Quays, London E14 4JP

Distributed in the United States of America by
Sterling Publishing Co., Inc.,
387 Park Avenue South, New York, NY 10016-8810

A CIP catalogue record for this book is available from the
British Library.

ISBN 1 84403 225 6

Photographs by Neil Barclay
Prop Styling by Fanny Ward
Food Styling by Pippa Cuthbert
Design by Austin Taylor
Jacket design and Art Direction by Jo Knowles
Publishing Manager Anna Cheifetz
Edited by Michelle Pickering

Printed in China

CONTENTS

বারের মজাই আলাদা

You can't beat the goodness of fresh food

INTRODUCTION

Indian food is a multicultural fusion of different cooking styles influenced by Muslims, Hindus, Moguls, Kashmiris, Punjabis, Goans and Bengalis, to name but a few. This book features a diverse range of recipes from all over the vast subcontinent of India – from north to south, east to west and Pakistan to Bangladesh.

I learned to cook from my grandmother. As a child, I'd often sit in her kitchen, watching her take ordinary ingredients and turn them into extraordinary mouth-drooling curries. It seemed like magic. Her wise hands knew just how much spice to add at any given moment.

Many people hold back from learning how to cook Indian food because the many different cooking styles and ingredients can seem daunting. The key to success lies in the **preparation**. When I cook, I always prepare my spices in advance, laid out on the table in a logical and regimented style. The recipes in this book use the same approach, so that anyone can achieve success, whatever their level of experience.

Each of the recipes in this book provides a list of ingredients. All of the ingredients that are added to the dish at the same time and cooked in the same way have been grouped together and numbered **bowl 1, bowl 2, bowl 3** and so on. Simply prepare all of the bowls of ingredients in advance, then start cooking. By organising the ingredients in this way, you don't have to worry about forgetting anything or adding something at the wrong time – all you have to do is transfer the relevant bowl of ingredients to your cooking utensil when indicated in the step-by-step instructions. It's a bit like learning to paint by numbers as a child, only this time you **cookbynumbers**. By mixing the ingredients in the right way and in the right order, you will get a successful result every time.

Whether this is your first experience of cooking Indian food or you are an accomplished cook wanting to learn a new cuisine, this book will help you make a wide variety of authentic Indian dishes easily and successfully time and time again.

Mahboob Momen

About the Recipes

All the recipes in this book have been graded to help you cook with confidence. Those with one chef's hat are extremely easy to make, those with more hats are more complex or take longer to prepare, but are still simple to if you follow the clear instructions. The chillies indicate the level of spiciness. You can adapt recipes to suit your taste by increasing or decreasing the amounts of chilli used.

 MORE COMPLEX

MODERATE

EASY

 HOT

MODERATE

MILD

VERY MILD

Equipment

There's no special equipment needed to cook Indian food, but the following make a good basic kit:

- Food processor
- Mortar and pestle – ideally a deep one
- Bowls for preparing the ingredients
- Mixing bowls – large, medium and small
- Good-quality saucepans with heavy bases
- Sharp knives
- Slotted spoons and wooden spoons
- Chopping board
- Rolling pin
- Colander
- Coffee grinder, to grind spices
- Traditional, heavy-based karahi (two-handled wok-style pan) or a wok for stir frying dishes over a high heat

Ingredients

As well as some basic equipment, most of which can be found in any family kitchen, you may find it useful to stock some of the ingredients that are used widely in Indian cookery. You can buy them from supermarkets or Indian grocers. As in any cooking, the end result is only as good as the food you use, so always buy the freshest ingredients possible.

COCONUT This is used in both sweet and savoury dishes. Fresh coconut is ideal, but you can use desiccated coconut instead. Some dishes require coconut milk. Buy it canned or make some up from dried powder. Creamed coconut comes in block form and adds a rich flavour to sauces.

GARLIC Large quantities of garlic give Indian cooking its rich, rounded flavours. Always use fresh garlic: test the bulb by pressing it gently; it should be firm to the touch and tightly held

Cookbynumbers demystifies the cooking process. The technique uses fresh ingredients, basic equipment and a simple method to enable you to cook delicious, authentic Indian food. Before you start cooking, you may find it useful to learn about some of the ingredients, equipment and techniques that commonly feature in Indian cooking.

HOW TO COOKBYNUMBERS

together. Garlic and ginger are used in so many recipes that it is worth making and freezing some garlic and ginger purée. Peel large quantities of roughly equal amounts of garlic and ginger and purée them in a blender. Put the mixture into ice-cube trays and freeze them for use at a later date. Garlic, ginger and onions are the basis of a good curry sauce.

GHEE This traditional Indian cooking fat is made from butter that has been heated and clarified, with any impurities skimmed off. It is used in very small quantities and stores well in the fridge.

KEWRA WATER This lovely perfumed water, made from a type of cactus, gives a flowery fragrance to all sorts of dishes, from rice to ice cream.

MASOOR DAL These red split lentils are probably the most commonly used pulse in Indian cooking. They are an integral part of dhansak curries and dal mixtures.

MOOLI This large, white radish root is not as hot as horseradish or red salad radishes but has a tangy flavour and crunchy texture that works well if used raw and grated. It also gives a bite to cooked dishes.

MOONG BEANS These little green beans are just one of the many types of pulse used in Indian cuisine. They have a nutty flavour and, unlike many pulses, are easy on the digestion.

OIL Use a good cooking oil such as sunflower oil, especially if you are cholesterol conscious. Olive oil is used for some recipes, but it is expensive and prone to burning if the cooking process needs the oil to get very hot. Use mustard oil when you want to create a really hot flavour in a dish.

OKRA These pointed green pods are a popular vegetable accompaniment. It is essential to buy them really fresh, as tired ones do not have the same crisp texture.

ONIONS You can use any onions but red onions give an extra sweet, strong flavour. The colour of a curry depends on how much you brown the onion when you fry it. I like to fry onions until they are golden brown and fairly dark. Some chefs fry their onions then whiz them in a blender to produce a smooth, dark brown onion liquid that makes an amazing sauce when cooked.

RICE Indian dishes are traditionally accompanied by basmati rice. Easy-cook basmati requires minimal cooking time (you can can use long grain easy-cook rice instead if you prefer).

TAMARIND This rich, sour-tasting pod is best bought in either concentrated or pulped form, to save all the tedious preparation. Used cooked and as an accompaniment, tamarind makes a delicious and tangy sauce.

WHITE RADISH see mooli.

YOGHURT Indians eat a lot of yoghurt, on its own, mixed into accompanying raitas and cooked in curries. It provides a soothing balance to the heat of chillies. The creamy texture and slightly sour taste are an essential part of many dishes; you can use low-fat varieties if you prefer.

ANISEED POWDER This is not one of the most commonly used spices in Indian cuisine, but if you can find some it will add a unique flavour to sweet and sour dishes.

ASAFOETIDA This is most commonly available as a powder made from a plant root. Also known as 'devil's dung', its name comes from the Latin *foetidus* – stinking. When raw it smells of rotting onions and tastes like concentrated rotting garlic, but when cooked the smell vanishes to produce a delicious taste of onions.

BAY LEAVES These richly aromatic leaves are regularly used in the early frying stages of many savoury Indian dishes and then removed.

BLACK SALT (kala nemak) This rock salt is actually reddish-grey, not black, due to its mineral and iron content. It is available as a block or ground and has a distinctive smoky flavour.

CARDAMOM Unless you buy it ground, cardamom pods are green, white or brown, according to their variety. They are used whole or with the seeds removed and provide an aromatic but not hot flavour. For a stronger flavour, remove the seeds and crush them before cooking. Unless stated otherwise, green cardamom is used in the recipes in this book.

CHILLIES Hot stuff, however you look at them. Chillies come in all shapes, colours and sizes but, as a rule, the smaller and thinner the chilli, the hotter the flavour. You can get chillies fresh, dried (whole or crushed) or ground to a powder. Green chillies are generally milder than red varieties but you can reduce the heat by removing and discarding the seeds. If you handle fresh chillies, it is vital to remember to wash your hands thoroughly afterwards – and whatever you do, don't touch your eyes. When adding chillies to recipes, err on the side of caution until you understand your level of tolerance for hot food.

CINNAMON This brown bark can be bought whole or in powdered form (some Indians call it pea sugar). The powdered form provides the most flavour in cooked dishes.

CLOVES Whole or ground cloves add a slightly medicinal flavour to food. Cloves are usually used whole in Indian dishes, with the flavour developed in the early spice-frying stages of the recipe.

CORIANDER This is a wonderfully versatile, aromatic spice that, in its fresh leaf form, is an essential last-minute garnish and a delicious herb to use in salads and accompaniments. In its seed form (available whole or ground), it is widely used to give body to curry sauces. Most supermarkets now stock fresh coriander but, if you cannot get regular supplies, buy it in bulk and freeze it. All you have to do is cut off and discard the roots, then wash the leaves and stalks. When dry, chop them up and store them in bags in the freezer. You do not need to defrost them before adding them to recipes.

CUMIN This aromatic spice adds a distinctive flavour but is not hot. It is available as whole seeds, black (roasted) seeds or ground, and is an essential ingredient in many savoury dishes and accompaniments.

Indian cookery utilises a wide variety of spices to create richly flavoured, mouth-watering dishes. You will find most of the spices are widely available and stocked on your local supermarket shelves. The few that aren't can be found in Indian grocers. Most recipes use the same range of spices, so you can gradually expand your storecupboard.

INDIAN SPICE CUPBOARD

FENUGREEK This spice has a powerful and pungent flavour and is available either as whole seeds (which should be lightly roasted before using) or ground to a powder. The aroma is fairly strong and similar to that of aniseed or burnt sugar.

GARAM MASALA Garam means hot and masala means spice, but the effect is generally spicy rather than hot. It is a blend of ground spices – many Indian families have their own jealously guarded recipe, but you can buy it readymade. It typically contains cloves, cardamom, coriander and cumin. To make your own, follow my mother's recipe: dry fry 1 tablespoon each of coriander seeds and cumin seeds and $\frac{1}{2}$ tablespoon each of whole cumin (broken into pieces), cloves, green cardamoms and black peppercorns in a pan over a medium heat until the spices are slightly crisp and browned. Allow them to cool, then grind in a coffee grinder or with a pestle and mortar.

GINGER The fresh root adds a wonderfully aromatic, spicy heat to savoury dishes and, in powdered form, gives a unique bite to baked sweet dishes. Although available as a dry powder, it is always best to use fresh. If you have time, you can provide yourself with a store-cupboard supply: simply peel and grate a good quantity of fresh ginger, pack it loosely into ice-cube trays and then freeze it to use whenever you need ginger in a hurry.

GREEN MANGO POWDER (amchoor) You can add a tangy, fruity flavour to sauces and snacks with green mango powder. It is made from unripe green mangoes that have been sun-dried and then very finely ground.

MACE This is the dried outer casing of the nutmeg and has a similar but slightly milder flavour.

MUSTARD SEEDS These tiny black seeds have a hot, spicy flavour that is released when fried, when they spit, hiss and pop.

NUTMEG The flavour of ground nutmeg deteriorates quickly, so it is best to keep whole nutmegs and grate them as needed.

PANCHFORAN This is a special spice mix used in some vegetable recipes. To make it, combine 1 teaspoon each of cumin seeds, aniseeds and fenugreek seeds with $\frac{1}{2}$ teaspoon each of mustard seeds and black cumin seeds. Mix them thoroughly and store in an airtight container.

PAPRIKA Use this ground red pepper to add a rich, spicy flavour to meat.

POPPY SEEDS Poppy seeds add a rich, nutty flavour to curry dishes.

SAFFRON These little orange strands are the dried stigma of the crocus flower. It takes a quarter million flowers to make just one pound of saffron, making it the most expensive spice in the world. Luckily, you only need to use a small quantity.

TURMERIC This bright yellow ground spice is made from the root of a plant of the ginger family, grown predominantly in India. It has a dry, hot, bitter taste, so it is never used in large quantities. This is the one that makes your fingers yellow if you eat with your hands.

Cooking Styles

India is home to a diverse range of cooking styles. They may seem unfamiliar but, by following the easy methods described in this book, you will be able to enjoy them successfully.

BHUNA This style of cooking involves frying a spice paste in hot oil. It is important to get the oil very hot when cooking spices in order to take the hard edge off their taste and to develop their flavour.

BOGAR This method involves frying dry spices in very hot oil. Take your courage in both hands and let the spices sizzle until they seem almost burned. This will give you a rich, nutty flavour in the finished dish.

BHAJI This style involves frying the main ingredients in a small amount of oil and/or dry frying them with spices. All those familiar restaurant accompaniments called bhajis are dry fried in this way and, although they may make their own juices during cooking, there is no real sauce.

KORMA This style of cooking creates a mild dish with a smooth flavour. Ginger, onion, cardamom, cinnamon and natural yoghurt are common ingredients.

REZALA This is a type of korma-style cooking but with the addition of green chillies and ingredients such as saffron, pistachios and almonds. The chillies do not make rezala dishes hot because they are added at the final stage of cooking. The combined ingredients make a rich, creamy dish.

NIRAMISH This is a way of cooking mixed vegetables using a panchforan spice mix (page 11) with a little sugar and a limited amount of other spices, if any at all. Niramish dishes are sometimes garnished with freshly roasted and then ground cumin.

PULLAO Fine-flavoured basmati rice is usually cooked with ghee to create this style of rice. Hard spices such as cinnamon, cardamom and cloves are used and the rice can be garnished with raisins, almonds, pistachios, fried onions, fresh orange or sliced boiled eggs.

BIRIYANI This special kind of pullao is cooked with meat and is particularly popular as a wedding dish.

KHICHURI This is rice and lentils cooked with other meat, vegetable or fish ingredients.

Tips and Techniques

Aquiring a few basic tips and techniques will help you make delicious Indian dishes.

MARINATING It really is worth marinating ingredients for the full recommended time. If you allow 8 hours or overnight, you will give flavours a chance to permeate the meat, fish or poultry before you cook it, which makes all the difference to the taste of the finished dish. If you are short of time, you can take a shortcut and marinate for 2 hours or less, though the flavour will not be as rich.

COOKING WITH SPICES Some recipes require you to dry roast certain spices over a low heat before grinding them

None of the cooking techniques used in this book is difficult. By organising the ingredients into a number of bowls, each of which is added to the recipe in a logical order and cooked in a specific way, the various cooking processes have been simplified so that anyone can follow the recipe, without any specialist knowledge of Indian cooking styles.

INDIAN COOKING TECHNIQUES

into a powder. Make sure you cover the pan with a lid when frying spices such as cumin or mustard seeds. Take particular care when adding water to spices that are frying. Always take the pan off the heat before gradually adding the water. Stay a safe distance away from the pan and never peer into the pan in case the spices spit up in your face. Some dishes require the use of whole spices. You can either remove them from the dish once it is cooked, or simply ask people not to eat them.

COOKING WITH YOGHURT Yoghurt is more widely used than cream in Indian cooking. It is a healthy alternative and also less expensive. However, many people are afraid of cooking with yoghurt because they think it will curdle when added to the curry. There's no need to worry. The yoghurt may look as if it is curdling but it is not; it is cooking in a very Indian way. Make sure you whisk the yoghurt first before adding it and then take the pan off the heat and pour the yoghurt into the pan gradually, stirring continuously with a fork as you do so.

Cooking Rice

There are two ways of cooking perfect rice: the traditional way in a saucepan or the quick way using a microwave oven. Use easy-cook basmati rice or another type of easy-cook rice. Whichever method you use, always wash the rice in cold water and drain before cooking.

IN A SAUCEPAN Put the washed rice in a pan with plenty of cold water and bring to the boil. Reduce the heat and simmer for 10 minutes, checking occasionally to see how fast the rice is cooking. Continue to simmer, testing the rice regularly, until it is cooked to your taste. Drain the rice in a colander, cover with a plate and leave to drain. Place the rice in a heated ovenproof dish and fluff the grains with a fork.

IN A MICROWAVE Put the washed rice in an ovenproof dish with 2 cups of water to each cup of rice. Allow to soak for a minimum of 15 minutes

(longer is better). Add salt and butter to taste. Either cover with a plate or use clingfilm with a small vent at the side. Microwave on full power for 10 minutes (for a 750-watt machine; adjust to suit your oven if necessary), until the water has been absorbed by the rice. Fluff and separate the grains using a fork.

COOK'S TIPS You may need to wash the rice three or four times until the water is clear and not cloudy. Add a little lemon juice, butter or salt to the water to help keep the grains separate. After cooking, you can place the cooked rice in an ovenproof dish and bake it in a hot oven for 5–10 minutes, then fluff the rice with some butter and/or chopped coriander. You can also add a chicken stock cube dissolved in small amount of boiling water to the water used for cooking the rice.

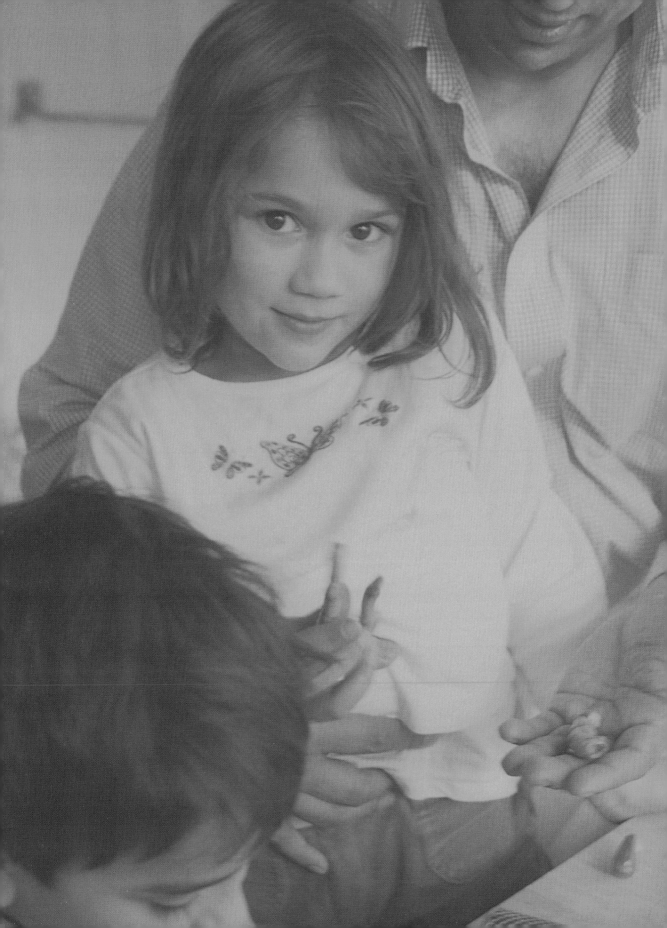

BITES, SIDES, BREADS AND RICE

1

Tandoori Chicken Bites
This is a simple but delicious recipe that you can make as a snack or starter. It's perfect for cooking on barbecues, too. Every family has their own Tandoori spice mix and this is my family's...

TANDOORI MURGH TUKRA

PREPARATION: 15–20 mins plus marinating overnight or minimum of 2 hours
COOKING: 30–40 mins
SERVES: 4 people

Ingredients

4 chicken legs, skinned and halved, or 8 chicken thighs or drumsticks, skinned

BOWL 1
600ml/1 pint natural yoghurt
2 red peppers, de-seeded and diced
4 cloves garlic, crushed
5cm/2in piece fresh ginger, peeled and grated
4 red chillies, trimmed and thinly sliced
2 medium onions, finely chopped
2 tablespoons chopped coriander leaves
juice of 2 lemons

BOWL 2
2 teaspoons ground coriander
2 teaspoons ground cumin
1 teaspoon freshly ground black pepper
1 teaspoon salt
½ teaspoon ground cinnamon
½ teaspoon celery salt
½ teaspoon fenugreek seeds
½ teaspoon grated nutmeg
4 bay leaves

The Day Before

• Make several deep cuts across the chicken flesh on each joint using a sharp knife. Set aside. Place **BOWL 1** in a blender and process to a smooth purée. Pour the purée into a large bowl, add **BOWL 2** and mix well. Add the chicken joints, turning to coat them all over with the marinade. Cover with clingfilm and leave in the fridge to marinate overnight.

To Cook

1 Preheat the oven to 180°C/350°F/Gas Mark 4. Remove the chicken from the marinade and place it in an ovenproof dish. Cover with foil and cook for 20–30 minutes, turning the pieces over 2 or 3 times to cook on all sides.

2 Remove the foil and cook for another 10 minutes, turning once to brown on both sides.

> **COOK'S TIPS** If you don't have time to marinate the chicken overnight, try to marinate it for at least 2 hours prior to cooking. Remember that the longer you marinate, the greater the taste and tenderness of the meat. To spice up your barbecues, remove the chicken from the marinade and cook it on the barbecue grill. Keep some of the marinade to baste the chicken joints if they get too dry while they cook.
> **SERVING SUGGESTIONS** Serve on their own as a snack or with a cool cucumber and tomato salad (page 32).

Spicy Kebabs
Kebab means shaped meat. These kebabs can be made from fresh minced beef or lamb and are delicious as a snack or starter, or served with a salad.

PREPARATION: 30 mins
COOKING: 10–20 mins
SERVES: 8–10 people

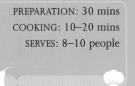

MUSHALLAR KABABS

Ingredients

225g/8oz red potatoes (such as Desirée), peeled, boiled and mashed

4 tablespoons sunflower oil

BOWL 1

750g/1½lb lean minced beef or lamb

1 onion, finely chopped

4 cloves garlic, crushed

2.5cm/1in piece fresh ginger, peeled and grated or finely chopped

2 tablespoons chopped coriander leaves

1 green chilli, de-seeded and finely chopped

1½ teaspoons salt

1 teaspoon garam masala

2 teaspoons ground coriander

2 teaspoons ground cumin

½ teaspoon chilli powder

1 teaspoon freshly ground black pepper

2 eggs, beaten

To Cook

1 Mix the mashed potato with **BOWL 1**, using your hands.

2 Form the mixture into 5cm/2in round patties and place them on a tray or board.

3 Heat the oil in a large, heavy-based frying pan and fry the patties, a few at a time if the pan is not large enough. Cook for 5–10 minutes on each side, turning when golden brown. When cooked through, lift out the patties and drain on absorbent paper.

COOK'S TIPS To make well-formed patties, take a little bit of the meat mixture in your hands. Cup your hands and roll them together, each hand in the opposite direction. You can prepare the meat mixture beforehand but the patties are best cooked immediately before serving. Add more chillies if you prefer a hotter taste.

SERVING SUGGESTIONS Serve as a starter with salad and a yoghurt dressing, or make smaller patties as a snack served with a chutney sauce as a dip.

Meat and Vegetable Kebabs

Shashlik means meat and vegetables on a skewer. It is a straightforward recipe that you can cook under the grill or on a barbecue.

PREPARATION: 10–15 mins plus marinating overnight or minimum of 2 hours
COOKING: 15–25 mins
SERVES: 4 people

SHASHLIK

Ingredients

2 chicken breasts, skinned and cut into 16 chunky cubes
1 large red onion, cut into chunks
$\frac{1}{2}$ red pepper, de-seeded and cut into chunks
$\frac{1}{2}$ green pepper, de-seeded and cut into chunks
$\frac{1}{2}$ yellow or orange pepper, de-seeded and cut into chunks
1 lime or small lemon, cut into wedges
4 green chillies, topped and tailed

BOWL 1

300ml/$\frac{1}{2}$ pint natural yoghurt
3 cloves garlic, crushed
2.5cm/1in piece fresh ginger, peeled and minced
1 teaspoon ground coriander
1 teaspoon ground cumin
1 teaspoon turmeric
1 teaspoon paprika
1 teaspoon garam masala
$\frac{1}{2}$ teaspoon freshly ground black pepper
$\frac{1}{2}$ teaspoon chilli powder
1$\frac{1}{2}$ teaspoons salt

The Day Before

• Mix **BOWL 1** to make the marinade. Add the chicken pieces, stir to coat and leave to marinate overnight.

To Cook

1 Remove the chicken pieces from the marinade and place on a sheet of foil on the grill pan. Preheat the grill to hot and cook the pieces for 10–15 minutes, turning once or twice to cook on all sides.

2 Remove the chicken pieces from the grill and let them cool a little.

3 Thread four pieces of chicken onto each skewer, interspersed with red onion chunks, red, green and yellow pepper chunks, a wedge of lemon or lime and a whole chilli. Make four kebabs.

4 Place the skewers under the grill and cook for another 5–10 minutes until sizzling hot and the vegetable pieces are starting to brown at the edges.

> **COOK'S TIPS** Try this recipe with diced lamb instead, allowing a little longer for cooking. You can also use different vegetables if you want. If using bamboo skewers, soak them in water for 30 minutes before threading them up to prevent them from burning under the grill. The kebabs can also be cooked on the barbecue. Simply cook the meat first on the skewers over the barbecue and then add the vegetables.
>
> **SERVING SUGGESTIONS** Serve with a cucumber and tomato salad (page 32) or onion and tomato salad (page 27), with a mint and yoghurt raita (page 38).

Skewered Mince Meat
Shikh kababs are minced meat shaped onto skewers and roasted over a flame or under a grill. They make a handy starter or a great light meal served with a salad.

PREPARATION: 15–20 mins
COOKING: 20 mins
SERVES: 4–6 people

KEEMAR SHIKH KABABS

Ingredients

BOWL 1

1kg/2lb lean minced lamb
2 teaspoons chilli powder
2 teaspoons salt

BOWL 2

1 teaspoon ground brown cardamom
2 eggs, lightly beaten
½ teaspoon black cumin seeds
1 teaspoon ground saffron
2 handfuls finely chopped coriander leaves
1 teaspoon dried mint

To Cook

1 Mix **BOWL 1** thoroughly and stir in **BOWL 2**.
2 Mix well, using your hands, and divide into 4–6 equal portions.
3 Mould each portion onto a bamboo skewer to make a sausage shape about 15cm/6in long.
4 Use your hands to smooth the surface of the kebabs, then grill or cook on a barbecue for about 20 minutes until cooked through.

COOK'S TIPS Moisten your hands with ice-cold water before applying the meat mixture to the skewers. You will find that the kebabs will stick less to your hands. Moisten your hands again when smoothing the outer surface of the kebabs. If using bamboo skewers, remember to soak them in water before use so that they don't burn during cooking.
SERVING SUGGESTION Ideal as a starter.

Vegetable or Meat Samosas

This popular snack is not difficult to make. For vegetarian samosas, use a pea and potato filling (page 114) or dry hot potato (page 125) omitting the tomatoes. For meat samosas, use a minced meat with peas filling (page 62). The filling must be a dry curry or the samosas will not 'hold'.

PREPARATION: 25–30 mins
COOKING: 15–20 mins
SERVES: 4–6 people

SAMOSAS

Ingredients

50g/2oz margarine
2 tablespoons natural yoghurt
plain flour for dusting
vegetarian or meat filling (see above)
6 tablespoons sunflower oil

BOWL 1
100g/4oz plain flour
½ teaspoon baking powder
½ teaspoon freshly ground black pepper
½ teaspoon cumin seeds
½ teaspoon salt

To Cook

1 Mix **BOWL 1** and rub the margarine into these ingredients flour using the fingertips until the mixture resembles fine breadcrumbs.

2 Add the yoghurt and mix thoroughly, using your hands to form a firm but fairly moist dough.

3 Shape the dough into 9–10 small balls, roughly 2.5cm/1in in diameter.

4 Roll out each ball of dough on a very lightly floured board to form a circle. The dough should be wafer thin.

5 Dust each circle of dough with flour and pile them on top of each other. Cut the pile of dough circles in half to give 18–20 half circles.

6 Taking one half circle at a time, place about a dessertspoonful of filling in the centre, then fold the samosa into a triangular cone shape with each side overlapping. Seal the open end by folding the dough over and sealing it with a little water.

7 Heat the oil in a saucepan until it is sizzling. Fry the samosas, turning once so they are golden brown on each side but not burned.

8 Remove from the pan and drain on absorbent paper.

COOK'S TIPS If the dough is too dry, add a little water until you obtain a firm consistency. Don't worry if the circles you roll out are not perfectly round, as you will eventually be making triangles. Check that the oil is sizzling hot by putting a tiny bit of bread into it. If the bread sizzles and floats to the surface, the oil is ready.
SERVING SUGGESTIONS Serve as a snack or with an aperitif, as a nice change from peanuts or Bombay mix.

Onion Bhajis

Bhaji is a style of cooking, literally meaning to fry with spices. This quick and easy dish is probably the most popular starter served in Indian restaurants.

PIAZ BHAJIS

Ingredients

sunflower oil for shallow frying

BOWL 1

4 tablespoons gram flour
2 large onions, thinly sliced
1 teaspoon salt
2 handfuls chopped coriander leaves
2 green chillies, trimmed and chopped

BOWL 2

½ teaspoon turmeric
½ teaspoon ground cumin
½ teaspoon chilli powder
½ teaspoon garam masala

To Cook

1 Mix **BOWL 1** thoroughly.
2 Stir in **BOWL 2**, adding in 1 tablespoon of water at a time, until you have created a loose, sticky dough.
3 Heat the oil in a deep frying pan until it is sizzling hot.
4 Carefully drop spoonfuls of the onion bhaji mixture into the oil and fry gently for 10–15 minutes until golden brown.
5 Lift out of the oil with a slotted spoon and drain on absorbent paper.

COOK'S TIPS Test whether the oil is hot enough by dropping in a small piece of bread. It will sizzle and float straight to the surface when the oil is ready. If you want to cook the bhajis in advance for a dinner party, let them cool and then quickly refry them for 1–2 minutes (without burning them) before serving.
SERVING SUGGESTIONS Onion bhajis are perfect as a starter or even a tasty snack.

Chicken Tikka
Chicken tikka is an essential ingredient for chicken tikka masala (page 89). On its own it makes a tasty dish and is also great as a starter.

MURGH TIKKA

Ingredients

750g/1½lb chicken breasts (approximately 4 breasts), skinned and cut into 4cm/1½in cubes
1 lemon, cut into wedges

BOWL 1

600ml/1 pint natural yoghurt
3 cloves garlic, crushed
juice of 2 lemons
2.5cm/1in piece fresh ginger, peeled and grated or finely chopped
1 teaspoon salt
2 red chillies, finely chopped (optional)
1 tablespoon olive oil

BOWL 2

2 teaspoons garam masala
2 teaspoons paprika
1 tablespoon ground coriander
½ teaspoon ground cumin

The Day Before

• Place the chicken in a large bowl and add **BOWL 1**, mixing thoroughly. Stir in **BOWL 2**, mix well, cover and leave to marinate overnight in the fridge.

To Cook

1 Preheat the oven to 200°C/400°F/Gas Mark 6. Lift the chicken pieces out of the marinade, draining off as much as possible. (Reserve the marinade if you are making chicken tikka masala.)
2 Arrange the chicken pieces on a roasting tray and cook for 10–15 minutes, turning once to cook evenly and draining off any excess liquid that collects.
3 When the chicken is tender and well browned on the outside, remove from the heat and garnish with lemon wedges.

COOK'S TIPS Take care not to overcook the chicken or it will become chewy.
SERVING SUGGESTION Makes a good starter served with onion and tomato salad (page 27) and mint and yoghurt raita (page 38).

Bengali Fish Patties
Bengal is a Hindu state in northeast India that shares its border and its most sacred river – the Ganges – with Bangladesh, now an independent Muslim state. Both regions share much of the same culinary tradition, with fish being an important part of the diet.

PREPARATION: 15–20 mins
COOKING: 10–15 mins
SERVES: 4 people

BENGALI MAS KOPTA

Ingredients

750g/1½lb fleshy fish, such as cod or haddock, skin removed and cut into 2.5cm/1in chunks

225g/8oz potatoes, peeled, boiled and mashed

1 small onion, finely chopped

2 tablespoons chopped coriander leaves

1 egg

3 tablespoons sunflower oil

BOWL 1

3 cloves garlic, crushed

2.5cm/1in piece fresh ginger, peeled and minced

2 green chillies, topped, tailed and finely chopped

1½ teaspoons ground coriander

1½ teaspoons ground cumin

1 teaspoon chilli powder

1 teaspoon turmeric

1 teaspoon salt

To Cook

1 Place the fish in a saucepan, cover with water and bring to the boil. Simmer for 5 minutes or so until the fish is cooked. Drain and set aside to cool.

2 Flake the cooked fish in a bowl and mix well with the mashed potato.

3 Add the onion, coriander and **BOWL 1** and mix thoroughly.

4 Add the egg and mix well to bind together.

5 Form small patties with the mixture (3–4cm/1–1½in diameter) and place them on a board, ready for cooking.

6 Heat the oil in a frying pan and gently fry the fish patties for 5–10 minutes, turning once, until cooked and golden brown.

> **COOK'S TIPS** Make sure you bind all the ingredients together thoroughly so that the patties don't fall apart when cooked. Use more or fewer green chillies, according to personal preference.
> **SERVING SUGGESTIONS** Serve the patties as a snack on their own or as a starter with a cucumber and tomato salad (page 32).

Bengali Spicy Omelette This is another dish that is often eaten by Indian people at breakfast. It is very easy to make.

PREPARATION: 15 mins
COOKING: 10 mins
SERVES: 2–4 people

BENGALI DIM BHAJI

Ingredients

4 or 5 eggs, beaten
3 tablespoons sunflower oil

BOWL 1

1 onion, thinly sliced
2 handfuls chopped coriander leaves
$\frac{1}{2}$ teaspoon turmeric
$\frac{1}{2}$ teaspoon cumin powder
$\frac{1}{2}$ teaspoon coriander powder
$\frac{1}{2}$ teaspoon chilli powder
$\frac{1}{2}$ teaspoon freshly ground black pepper
$\frac{1}{2}$ teaspoon salt

To Cook

1 Mix **BOWL 1** thoroughly using your hands until the slices of onion are evenly covered with spices.
2 Add the eggs and mix again using your hands or a fork, but do not whisk it.
3 Heat the oil in a large frying pan. Add the egg mixture, cover and fry gently on one side for about 5 minutes until the omelette is firm.
4 Cut the omelette into four quarters and turn them over to cook on the other side for 5 minutes until firm.

COOK'S TIPS Instead of quartering the omelette, you could slide it onto a large plate, put the frying pan over it and turn over to cook on the other side. To give the omelette more substance, add parboiled potatoes and tomatoes so that it's a bit like a Spanish tortilla.
SERVING SUGGESTIONS This is a great dish for breakfast with a chapatti (page 42) or naan bread (page 44).

Onion and Tomato Salad
This recipe is ideal for anyone who loves onions and enjoys a salad with a fiery bite.

PREPARATION: 5 mins
COOKING: none
SERVES: 4 people

PIAZ O TOMETO

Ingredients

2 large onions, finely chopped
2 tomatoes, thinly sliced
1–2 tablespoons chopped coriander leaves
½ teaspoon salt
2 green chillies, finely chopped (optional)

To Cook

1 Mix the onions, tomatoes and coriander together in a bowl.
2 Add the salt, adjusting the quantity if necessary.
3 Stir in the chillies.

COOK'S TIPS Try red onions for a hotter taste.
SERVING SUGGESTIONS Serve with vegetable or meat curries.

Spiced Potato with Cashew Nuts

This wonderful little snack consists of boiled potatoes and roasted cashew nuts combined with fresh coriander and a special spice mix called chat masala.

ALOO CHAT

Ingredients

75g/3oz cashew nuts
8 medium potatoes, peeled, boiled and diced
2 large onions, chopped
6 green chillies, trimmed and chopped
6 tomatoes, skinned and chopped
handful chopped coriander leaves

BOWL 1
1½ tablespoons cumin seeds
½ teaspoon black peppercorns

BOWL 2
2 tablespoons dried mint
½ tablespoon asafoetida powder
½ teaspoon grated nutmeg

BOWL 3
2 tablespoons green mango powder (amchoor)
½ teaspoon paprika
½ teaspoon chilli powder
1 tablespoon black salt (kala namak)
½ teaspoon salt

To Cook

1 Dry roast the cashew nuts in a heavy-based frying pan for 2–3 minutes until golden brown all over. Chop roughly and set aside.

2 Dry roast **BOWL 1** in a heavy pan for 3–4 minutes to bring out the flavour of the spices.

3 Reduce to a low heat and add **BOWL 2**. Roast lightly for another 2 minutes.

4 Using a spice grinder (or a coffee mill or pestle and mortar), grind the mixture into a fine powder and then mix well with **BOWL 3**. This is the chat masala spice mix.

5 In a large bowl, mix the cashew nuts, potatoes, onions, green chillies, tomatoes and coriander. Add chat masala to taste and mix in well.

> **COOK'S TIPS** Create variations in texture and crunch by using roasted and chopped peanuts, puffed rice, or pomegranate seeds.
> **SERVING SUGGESTIONS** Makes a delicious starter, served plain or with tamarind and mint sauce (page 39).

Two-bean Salad

This is a wholesome and filling salad that can be eaten on its own or with some green lettuce. It is perfect for serving at summer buffet parties.

PREPARATION: 15 mins plus
soaking overnight
COOKING: 1¼ hours plus 1–2 hours chilling
SERVES: 4 people

TIN RAKAMER SIMER BICHI

Ingredients

225g/8oz black-eyed beans, soaked overnight in cold water
225g/8oz chickpeas, soaked overnight in cold water
225g/8oz can red kidney beans, rinsed and drained
juice of 1 lemon
small handful chopped coriander leaves

BOWL 1

1 clove garlic, crushed
1 tablespoon sesame oil
1 teaspoon ground cumin
1 teaspoon ground coriander
1 teaspoon freshly ground black pepper
1 teaspoon salt

BOWL 2

1 medium onion, finely chopped
2 green chillies, trimmed and cut into 5mm/¼in slices

To Cook

1 Drain the beans and chickpeas, put them in a large saucepan and cover with fresh water. Bring to the boil, then simmer gently for 1 hour until the beans and peas are cooked and tender but not mushy. Drain and set aside to cool.

2 Mix **BOWL 1** thoroughly and stir in **BOWL 2**.

3 Add the black-eyed beans, chickpeas and red kidney beans. Mix well.

4 Pour over the lemon juice, add the coriander and mix well.

5 Adjust the seasoning if necessary, then chill for couple of hours.

COOK'S TIPS You could use dried red kidney beans instead of canned, but make sure you soak them well and cook them thoroughly because they are poisonous in their raw state. Alternatively, you could use cans of black-eyed beans and chickpeas to save time. Be careful not to crush the beans when you stir the salad or you'll end up with a mashed bean salad. Omit the green chillies for a milder taste.

SERVING SUGGESTIONS Serve on its own as a healthy vegetarian snack or at barbecues as an alternative salad.

Cucumber Salad with Peanuts
This salad, with its sour taste and crunchy texture, is very refreshing but also has a bit of a bite.

SHASHA O BADAMER

Ingredients

1 large onion, chopped
4 green or red chillies, trimmed and chopped
100g/4oz peanuts, coarsely chopped
2 tomatoes, skinned and chopped
1 green pepper, de-seeded and chopped
2 handfuls chopped coriander leaves
1 tablespoon vinegar
1 tablespoon olive oil
½ teaspoon sugar
½ teaspoon salt

To Cook

1 Mix all the ingredients together in a bowl.
2 Adjust the seasoning if necessary.

COOK'S TIPS Remember to check if any of your guests are allergic to nuts before serving this salad.
SERVING SUGGESTION This is great as a side dish at a dinner party.

Cucumber and Tomato Salad
This popular salad is often served as a 'cooler' with hotter dishes. You can also spice it up with some chillies to make a salsa-style salad.

PREPARATION: 10 mins
COOKING: none
SERVES: 4 people

SHASHA O TOMETO

Ingredients

1 cucumber, diced or cut into thin sticks
4 tomatoes, skinned and diced
1 large red onion, finely chopped
1–2 tablespoons chopped coriander leaves
½ teaspoon sugar
½ teaspoon salt

To Cook

1 Mix the cucumber, tomatoes, red onion and coriander in a salad bowl.
2 Add the sugar and salt, adjusting the quantities to taste if necessary.

COOK'S TIPS If you prepare this salad in advance, don't add the sugar and salt until ready to serve or the salad will go watery. Spice it up with some finely sliced green or red chillies.
SERVING SUGGESTIONS Serve as a cooling accompaniment to curries. Dress the salad with a teaspoon or so of tamarind and mint sauce (page 39) if you wish.

Red Lentils

Lentils, or dal are the basis of most Indian diets, both vegetarian and non-vegetarian, and Indian meals often begin with dal and rice. Keep some in the freezer to eat on its own as a soup in the evening. This recipe is for a relatively thick dal.

PREPARATION: 10–15 mins
COOKING: 55–70 mins
SERVES: 4–6 people

MASOOR DAL

Ingredients

225g/8oz red split lentils, well rinsed and drained

4 tablespoons sunflower or olive oil

2 tomatoes, washed and roughly chopped

1½ teaspoons salt

BOWL 1

1 medium onion, peeled and thinly sliced

2 cloves garlic, peeled and crushed

BOWL 2

2 teaspoons ground coriander

2 teaspoons ground cumin

2 teaspoons turmeric

½ teaspoon chilli powder

4 cloves

4 cardamom pods

5cm/2in cinnamon stick

To Cook

1 Place the lentils in a saucepan with 600ml/1 pint water and bring to the boil.

2 Reduce the heat, cover and simmer gently for 20–30 minutes or until the lentils break down and have a soupy consistency. Set aside.

3 Heat the oil in a saucepan and fry **BOWL 1** for 3–5 minutes until the onion begins to caramelise and turn golden brown

4 Add **BOWL 2** and continue to fry for 1 minute, stirring continuously to make sure that the mixture does not stick to the pan and that the spices do not burn.

5 Add the cooked lentils (with any liquid they have been boiled in) and stir thoroughly, mixing well with the onion and spices. Simmer for 5 minutes.

6 Add the tomatoes and salt, stir and simmer for another 10–15 minutes until the tomatoes are soft. Adjust the seasoning if necessary.

COOK'S TIPS Wash the lentils thoroughly in several changes of water before boiling. Make sure they are covered with water before cooking and remove any white foam from the surface of the boiling water with a spoon. If the dal is too thick, add a little water with the tomatoes and salt.

SERVING SUGGESTIONS Serve with rice and vegetables for a nutritious vegetarian meal, or eat on its own with a chapatti (page 42) or naan bread (page 44) and salad as a late evening snack.

Bombay Duck Mix

Shuthki – or Bombay duck (dried fish) as it is also known – is a very cheap and popular food in India. It also makes an interesting chutney.

PREPARATION: 15–20 mins plus soaking overnight
COOKING: 1½–1¾ hours
SERVES: 6–10 people

SHUTHKI BHARTA

Ingredients

225g/8oz Bombay duck
2 tablespoons vinegar
4 tablespoons mustard oil
8 red chillies, trimmed and chopped

BOWL 1

2 teaspoons cumin seeds
1 teaspoon mustard seeds

BOWL 2

1 onion, thinly sliced
4 cloves garlic, thinly sliced

BOWL 3

2 teaspoons garam masala
2 teaspoons paprika
½ teaspoon mango powder (amchoor)
1 teaspoon turmeric
1 teaspoon ground cumin
1 teaspoon ground coriander
1 teaspoon chilli powder

BOWL 4

2 tablespoons sugar
2 tablespoons tomato purée

The Day Before

• Place the Bombay duck in a shallow bowl with the vinegar and just enough water to cover. Cover with clingfilm and leave to soak overnight.

To Cook

1 Preheat the oven to 180°C/350°F/Gas Mark 4. Heat the oil in a large saucepan, add **BOWL 1** and fry for 1–2 minutes.
2 Add **BOWL 2** and continue to fry for 3–5 minutes until the onion is turning golden brown.
3 Add **BOWL 3** and fry for 5–10 minutes, stirring occasionally, until the onion is tender.
4 Stir in **BOWL 4** and continue to fry, stirring regularly, for another 5 minutes.
5 Add the Bombay duck with the soaking liquid and bring to the boil, then simmer for 15–20 minutes.
6 Strain off any excess liquid and stir in the chillies. Transfer the mixture to an ovenproof dish, cover and cook for 1 hour.
7 Allow to cool, then place in a sterilised glass jar and cover with a tight-fitting lid. Store for a couple of months before eating.

COOK'S TIPS Make sure the Bombay duck is well broken up into small pieces when cooking. When correctly stored, the mix lasts almost forever.
SERVING SUGGESTION Goes well as an accompaniment with almost any dish if you like the strong, salty taste of dried fish.

Green Chilli Chutney Purée

This recipe uses a lot of chillies, so you can spice up any Indian dish with just a spoonful. It makes a delicious accompaniment to any Indian meal.

PREPARATION: 5–10 mins
COOKING: none
SERVES: 6–8 people

KACHA ACHAR

Ingredients

BOWL 1
750g/1½lb green chillies, trimmed
4 tablespoons vinegar
½ teaspoon salt
½ teaspoon sugar

BOWL 2
2 or 3 generous handfuls coriander, stems removed and leaves chopped
1 large onion, chopped

To Cook

1 Mix **BOWL 1** and allow the ingredients to marinate together for a few minutes, then transfer to a blender.
2 Add **BOWL 2** and blend until smooth.
3 Pour the purée into a sterilised glass jar, seal with a tight-fitting lid and store.

COOK'S TIPS You may want to add some thinly sliced fresh green chillies to make a more interesting chutney purée. When correctly stored, the purée will keep for several months.
SERVING SUGGESTION Goes with most dishes, assuming you like your food hot.

Mango Relish This relish is a delightful little accompaniment for dinner parties or just everyday eating.

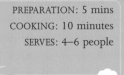

PREPARATION: 5 mins
COOKING: 10 minutes
SERVES: 4–6 people

AMER ACHAR

Ingredients

450g/1lb green mangoes, peeled, stoned and sliced
1 teaspoon salt
2 tablespoons chopped mint leaves

BOWL 1
2 teaspoons sugar
6 tablespoons vinegar
2.5cm/1in piece fresh ginger, peeled and finely sliced
2 red chillies, trimmed and finely sliced

To Cook

1 Mix the mango with the salt in a bowl and allow to stand for 3–4 minutes.

2 Rinse the mango thoroughly in cold water.

3 Place the mango in a saucepan with **BOWL 1**, bring to the boil and simmer for 8–10 minutes, stirring regularly. Set aside to cool.

4 Add the mint and mix well.

5 Pour the hot chutney into a sterilised glass jar. Cover with absorbent paper or muslin while it cools.

6 When completely cold, cover with a tight-fitting lid and store in a cool place.

COOK'S TIPS Add a few more chillies or even crushed dried chillies if you want to make a hot and spicy mango relish. When correctly stored, this relish will keep for up to 3 months.

SERVING SUGGESTIONS Great as an accompaniment to either snacks or main dishes.

Mint and Yoghurt Raita This is a wonderful accompaniment to cool the palate when eating spicy dishes.

PUDINA PATAR O DAHI RAITA

Ingredients

150ml/¼ pint natural yoghurt
2 tablespoons chopped coriander leaves

BOWL 1
1 tablespoon finely chopped mint leaves
½ teaspoon chilli powder
½ teaspoon garam masala
pinch of grated nutmeg
½ teaspoon salt
½ teaspoon sugar

To Cook

1 Place the yoghurt in a large bowl and whisk with a spoon until smooth.
2 Add **BOWL 1** and mix thoroughly.
3 Garnish with chopped coriander.

COOK'S TIPS If you prefer, leave out the chilli, garam masala and nutmeg for a less spicy dish.
SERVING SUGGESTION Works well as an accompaniment to most Indian dishes.

Tamarind and Mint Sauce
This fresh coriander and mint sauce has a deliciously tangy taste.

PREPARATION: 10 mins
COOKING: none
SERVES: 6–8 people

TETUL O PUDINA PATAR

Ingredients

BOWL 1

generous handful coriander leaves,
coarse stems removed

4–5 sprigs mint, coarse stems removed

4 cloves garlic, crushed

BOWL 2

1 tablespoon tamarind purée or concentrate

2 teaspoons sugar

$\frac{1}{2}$ teaspoon salt

To Cook

1 Place **BOWL 1** in a blender with 150ml/$\frac{1}{4}$ pint water and blend well.

2 Add **BOWL 2** and mix well.

COOK'S TIPS Buy tamarind purée from your local Indian grocers or make it by boiling fresh tamarind in water for 20–30 minutes and then sieving the contents to remove all seeds and husks.

SERVING SUGGESTIONS Serve with samosas (page 21), lentil pancakes (page 51) or spiced potato with cashew nuts (page 28).

Red Chilli Chutney with Mint
This is a very hot chutney for lovers of really hot food.

PREPARATION: 20–30 mins
COOKING: none
SERVES: 4–6 people

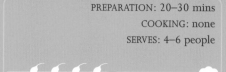

LAL MARICHER ACHAR

Ingredients

225g/8oz red chillies, trimmed and cut in half if long

225g/8oz mint leaves, stems removed and finely chopped

juice of 1 lime

2.5cm/1in piece fresh ginger, peeled and finely grated

½ teaspoon salt

½ teaspoon sugar

To Cook

1 Mix all of the ingredients together in a bowl.

2 Allow to stand for 10–20 minutes to let the flavours blend.

> **COOK'S TIPS** This recipe works just as well with green chillies but will create a less fiery chutney. It also stores well.
>
> **SERVING SUGGESTION** This chutney goes well with most dishes but be careful as it is very hot.

Chapatti

Chapatti is an Indian bread and forms a staple part of any Indian meal. It is easy to make and often used as an alternative to rice. Chapattis with leftover curries from the previous night make a delicious breakfast.

PREPARATION: 15 mins plus
30 mins resting
COOKING: 20 mins
SERVES: 6–8 people

ATA RUTI

Ingredients

plain flour for dusting

BOWL 1
750g/1½lb wholemeal flour
4 tablespoons plain flour

To Cook

1 Mix **BOWL 1** and add enough cold water (about 450ml/³/₄ pint) to make a flexible dough. Work this well with your hands, kneading on a floured surface until the dough is smooth and elastic. Cover with clingfilm and leave to rest for 30 minutes.

2 Knead again and pull off small balls of dough.

3 Dip each ball of dough into the plain flour and flatten out using a rolling pin.

4 Heat a griddle or large, heavy-based frying pan until very hot. Dry fry each chapatti for 10–20 seconds on each side.

5 Press lightly with a spatula to puff up the chapattis while cooking.

6 Cover the finished chapattis with a cloth to keep them warm while cooking the rest.

COOK'S TIPS When cooking chapattis, you will notice that brown spots appear on the underside. When this happens, turn over and dry fry the other side.

SERVING SUGGESTIONS Chapattis are at their best freshly cooked. Spread them with butter as you serve them. They are lovely to eat with any meat curry or lentils (pages 34 and 113).

Parata This is a richer version of the classic chapatti that is often eaten at breakfast.

PREPARATION: 25 mins plus
30 mins resting
COOKING: 20 mins
SERVES: 6–8 people

PARATA

Ingredients

750g/1½lb wholemeal flour plus
a little extra for rolling
50g/2oz margarine, cut into small pieces
225g/8oz ghee

To Cook

1 Place the flour in a large bowl, add the margarine and rub in using the fingertips until the mixture looks like fine breadcrumbs.

2 Slowly add water (about 200ml/7fl oz), mixing to make a smooth, flexible dough. Cover with clingfilm and leave to rest for 30 minutes.

3 Divide the dough into 16 equal portions and roll each into a ball.

4 Flatten a ball on a lightly floured surface to make a circle about 10cm/4in in diameter.

5 Smooth some ghee over the surface and then fold in half, keeping the ghee inside. Spread with more ghee, and fold again. Repeat for each round of dough.

6 When all are folded, roll each one out on a lightly floured surface to about 5mm/¼in thick.

7 Heat a large, heavy-based frying pan and spread some ghee over the surface. Cook each parata for about 30 seconds on each side, regreasing the pan between sides.

> **COOK'S TIPS** Cook each parata until it turns golden brown and brown spots appear on each side but do not burn.
> **SERVING SUGGESTIONS** Great with any vegetable or meat dish.

Naan Bread
Traditionally naans are baked in clay ovens. However, few people have clay ovens in their homes, so this recipe is designed to suit all kitchen capabilities.

PREPARATION: 15 mins plus
4 hours rising
COOKING: 20–30 mins
SERVES: 4–6 people

NAAN

Ingredients

plain flour for rolling
sunflower oil for greasing
100g/4oz butter
2 tablespoons poppy seeds

BOWL 1

350g/12oz plain flour
1 teaspoon salt
1½ teaspoons sugar
½ teaspoon baking powder

BOWL 2

15g/½oz fresh yeast mixed with
150ml/¼ pint warm milk
150ml/¼ pint natural yoghurt

To Cook

1 Mix **BOWL 1** thoroughly.

2 Add **BOWL 2** and stir it into the flour mixture to form a dough.

3 Knead well, then cover and leave to rise for around 4 hours.

4 Divide the dough into 10–12 equal portions and form into balls. On a floured surface, flatten the balls into teardrop shapes using your hands.

5 Using both hands, slap the naan from one hand to the other until you have a teardrop-shaped naan about the right size (slightly larger than your hands).

6 Heat a heavy-based frying pan and lightly grease it with oil. Cook the naan on one side, spread the uncooked side with butter and sprinkle poppy seeds over the surface. Heat this side under a grill.

> **COOK'S TIPS** Remove any jewellery from your hands when mixing the dough.
>
> **SERVING SUGGESTIONS** Naan goes well with most meat dishes and any type of vindaloo, including chicken vindaloo (page 88) and vegetable vindaloo (page 120).

Spiced Pullao Rice

This is a dish from the kitchens of the Mogul emperors. On special days of celebration when there were many people to entertain, the emperors needed a dish that could be produced cost effectively. Spiced pullao rice was invented as an exotic tasting dish that was easy and cheap to make.

PREPARATION: 15 mins
COOKING: 25–30 mins
SERVES: 4–6 people

MUSHALLAR PULLAO

Ingredients

175ml/6fl oz sunflower oil
1 medium onion, thinly sliced
450g/1lb basmati rice, washed thoroughly and well drained
1 teaspoon salt

BOWL 1
1 clove garlic, thinly sliced
10 cloves
10 cardamom pods
7.5cm/3in cinnamon stick

BOWL 2
100g/4oz sultanas
50g/2oz blanched almonds

To Cook

1 Heat all but 3 tablespoons of the oil in a large pan and fry the onion for about 5 minutes until soft and golden brown.
2 Add **BOWL 1** and continue to cook gently for 1–2 minutes to blend the flavours.
3 Add the rice and mix well. Continue to fry gently for 1–2 minutes, stirring so that the rice is covered with the spices and oil.
4 Add the salt and enough water to just cover the rice.
5 Bring to the boil, then cover the pan tightly, simmer and cook for another 10–15 minutes, checking every now and then, until the rice is tender and all the water has been absorbed.
6 Heat the remaining oil in a frying pan and shallow fry **BOWL 2** for 1–2 minutes, then add to the rice and mix in well.

COOK'S TIPS Make sure the rice is coated well with the spice mixture throughout cooking, and that the lid is on tightly when simmering the rice.

Spiced Rice with Pulses

This is a spiced rice dish with pulses that many say was made famous by the British Raj. The mix of spices and green chillies adds a special bite to this recipe that you will enjoy if you like a slightly hot dish. It also makes a tasty breakfast.

PREPARATION: 20 mins plus
30 mins soaking
COOKING: ½–2 hours
SERVES: 4–6 people

MUSHALLAR KHICHURI

Ingredients

3 tablespoons sunflower oil

1 onion, thinly sliced

450g/1lb basmati rice, washed and left to soak in plenty of cold water

4 green chillies, trimmed and split lengthways

handful chopped coriander leaves

BOWL 1

175g/6oz red lentils

75g/3oz chickpeas

75g/3oz moong beans

BOWL 2

2 bay leaves

2.5cm/1in piece fresh ginger, peeled and grated

2 cloves garlic, crushed

1 teaspoon turmeric

1 teaspoon chilli powder

2 teaspoons ground coriander

2 teaspoons ground cumin

To Cook

1 Place **BOWL 1** in a sieve and rinse. Return the pulses to the bowl, cover with water and allow to soak for 30 minutes.

2 Drain the pulses, place in a saucepan, cover with water and bring to the boil. Reduce the heat and simmer for 1 hour until the pulses are nearly cooked. Set aside.

3 Heat the oil in a large saucepan and fry the onion with **BOWL 2** for 2–3 minutes until the onion is just turning golden.

4 Drain the rice and add this to the saucepan, stir well and continue to cook for 2–3 minutes, mixing well with the spices.

5 Add the pulses along with the green chillies. Bring to the boil, then simmer for 10–20 minutes until the rice and pulses are cooked to your liking. I like the rice to be *al dente* but the pulses need to be properly cooked.

6 Garnish with coriander.

COOK'S TIPS Red lentils (masoor dal) are best for this recipe, although you could try other types.
SERVING SUGGESTION Goes well with a beef curry and chutney.

Vegetable and Fruit Pullao Rice This is a lovely main dish for vegetarians, and can be served as a highly nutritious and satisfying meal in itself.

PREPARATION: 30 mins plus
30 mins soaking
COOKING: 30–50 mins
SERVES: 4–6 people

SHABJI O FOL PULLAO

Ingredients

3 tablespoons sunflower oil

1 onion, thinly sliced

450g/1lb basmati rice, washed and left to soak in plenty of cold water for 30 minutes

BOWL 1

2 large carrots, peeled and diced

10 small cauliflower florets (about half a medium cauliflower)

2 courgettes, diced

100g/4oz shelled peas

BOWL 2

1 teaspoon cumin seeds

1 bay leaf

½ teaspoon ground ginger

pinch of ground mace

3 cloves

2 cardamom pods

BOWL 3

50g/2oz seedless grapes

1 firm mango, peeled, stoned and diced

1 small pineapple, peeled and diced

1 apple, peeled and diced

1 tablespoon cashew nuts

1 tablespoon blanched slivered or split almonds

1 tablespoon sultanas

To Cook

1 Place **BOWL 1** in a saucepan with enough water to cover and bring to the boil. Simmer gently for 3–5 minutes, then drain the vegetables well and set aside.

2 Heat the oil in a large frying pan, add the onion and fry gently for 5–10 minutes until golden brown.

3 Add **BOWL 2** and fry gently for 1–2 minutes, making sure the spices are well mixed into the oil.

4 Add the drained vegetables and fry for 3–4 minutes, mixing well with the spices.

5 Add **BOWL 3** and fry gently for 1–2 minutes.

6 Rinse the rice, drain and add to the pan, mixing well.

7 Cook for another 5–10 minutes until the rice is cooked through but the grains are still separate and flaky.

COOK'S TIPS If you wish, put the rice, vegetable, fruit and nut mixture into an ovenproof casserole dish and cook the last stage in a moderate oven – 180°C/350°F/Gas Mark 4 – for 5–10 minutes.
SERVING SUGGESTIONS Serve as a vegetarian dinner party dish or as a meal in itself.

Mango Rice This wonderful rice creation has a truly delicious flavour that is difficult to resist.

PREPARATION: 10 mins plus
30–40 mins soaking
COOKING: 25–30 mins
SERVES: 4–6 people

AAM BHAT

Ingredients

50g/2oz chickpeas, soaked in water for
30–40 minutes
225g/8oz basmati rice, rinsed in cold water
and drained
125ml/4fl oz sunflower oil
1 large mango, peeled and thinly sliced
2 red chillies, trimmed and chopped
handful chopped coriander leaves

BOWL 1

1 teaspoon ground turmeric
4 cloves
4 cardamom pods
2 teaspoons chilli powder

To Cook

1 Place the chickpeas and rice in a saucepan with 600ml/1 pint water, bring to the boil and simmer for 12–15 minutes until the rice and chickpeas are cooked *al dente*. Drain and set aside, keeping warm.

2 Heat the oil in a large frying pan, add **BOWL 1** and fry gently for 1–2 minutes.

3 Add the sliced mango and continue to fry for 1–2 minutes, mixing gently.

4 Stir in the drained rice and chickpeas with the chillies and mix well. Place in a warmed serving dish and garnish with coriander.

> **COOK'S TIPS** You could add sultanas or almonds to the rice to vary the texture and taste.
> **SERVING SUGGESTION** Serve with other vegetarian dishes to add some vegetable protein.

Lentil Pancakes
These pancakes stuffed with lightly spiced lentils make a delicious snack at any time of day.

PREPARATION: 30–45 mins
COOKING: 45–60 mins
SERVES: 4–6 people

DALPURI

Ingredients

2 red chillies, finely chopped
sunflower oil for shallow frying
½ medium onion, thinly sliced
handful mint leaves, finely chopped
750g/1½lb plain flour plus extra for rolling

BOWL 1

100g/4oz red lentils, well rinsed and drained
½ teaspoon ground ginger
2 teaspoons finely chopped onion
1 green chilli, finely chopped
1 teaspoon salt

To Cook

1 Put **BOWL 1** into a saucepan with 150ml/¼ pint water and bring to the boil. Cover and simmer for 15–20 minutes until all the water has been absorbed. Stir regularly until the lentils look dry and bind together in lumps. Set aside.

2 Fry the red chillies in a dash of oil for 2–3 minutes, then set aside until they become cool and crisp.

3 Heat another 2 tablespoons of the oil and fry the sliced onion until it is golden brown. Strain the oil from the onion and set the onion aside on a large plate, spread out, until it becomes cool and crisp.

4 Crush the fried red chillies and onion with a pestle and mortar. Add the mint and continue to crush to form a paste-like mixture. Add this to the lentils and mix well. Divide the mixture into 20 balls.

5 Mix the flour with a dash of oil and about 150ml/¼ pint water to make a dough. Add more or less water as necessary. Divide the dough into 20 balls, using your thumb to press a hole in the middle of each one so that they form 20 little cups.

6 Stuff each flour ball with a lentil ball and seal carefully.

7 Sprinkle flour onto a board and roll each ball, with the sealed part face down, into a small round pancake.

8 Fry the pancakes in oil until golden brown. Drain on absorbent paper.

> **COOK'S TIPS** Stir regularly to make sure the lentils mixture does not burn. Spread out the fried red chillies and onion so that they dry quickly. Use coriander if you cannot find mint leaves.
> **SERVING SUGGESTIONS** Serve hot with tamarind and mint sauce (page 39) or as a breakfast snack.

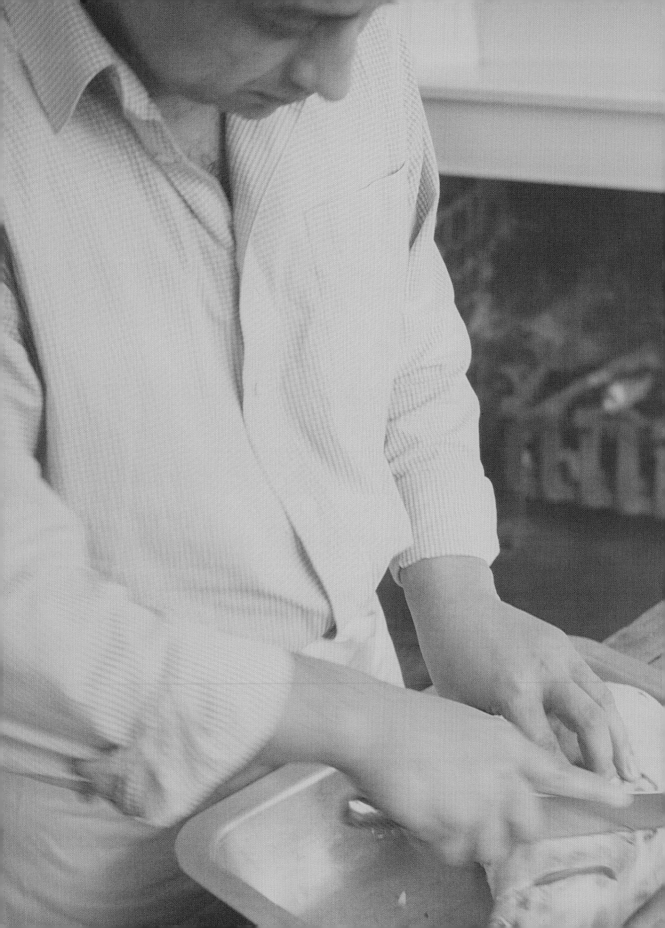

LAMB
AND
BEEF
2

Spicy Roast Leg of Lamb
This dish was created for grand feast days and uses two different masala mixes: one for marinating the meat to give it a deep flavour and to tenderise it before roasting; and the other for applying to the meat just before cooking to keep the joint moist while infusing extra flavour.

PREPARATION: 30–40 mins plus marinating overnight
COOKING: 2 hours
SERVES: 3–5 people

MUSHALLAR MESH RAAN

Ingredients

2.5kg/5½lb leg of lamb on the bone

BOWL 1
5 cardamom pods
10 cloves
5cm/2in cinnamon stick
1 teaspoon turmeric
1 teaspoon chilli powder
2 teaspoons ground cumin
2 large onions, chopped
5 cloves garlic, crushed
5cm/2in piece fresh ginger, peeled and chopped
juice of 2 lemons
1 tablespoon salt

BOWL 2
2 tablespoons natural yoghurt
1 tablespoon honey
1 tablespoon pistachio nuts
1 teaspoon raisins

The Day Before

- Trim any excess fat from the lamb and make several deep cuts along each side of the joint using a sharp knife. Place **BOWL 1** in a blender and process until smooth. Rub the mixture all over the lamb, pressing it into the cuts. Cover with clingfilm and leave to marinate overnight in the fridge.

To Cook

1 Grind **BOWL 2** using a pestle and mortar or a blender.
2 Preheat the oven to 180°C/350°F/Gas Mark 4. Place the lamb in a large roasting dish with the first masala mix and cover with the second masala mix.
3 Cover the roasting dish tightly with foil and cook for 1½ hours until the meat is almost cooked and tender.
4 Remove the foil and cook uncovered for 10–15 minutes so that the spice mix becomes crispy.

COOK'S TIPS Blending the ingredients of the first masala mix may be a bit messy and involve a lot of scraping down of the ingredients from the walls of the blender. Try not to add any water, but just continue to scrape down and get the smoothest paste possible. Increase the oven temperature, if need be, to ensure that the second masala mix goes crisp on top of the lamb. To check if the meat is cooked, prick it with a fork or sharp skewer. If the juices are clear (with no blood), the joint is cooked.
SERVING SUGGESTION Delicious served with rice and vegetables.

Red Meat Curry
Roghan gosht has its origins in Persia, many centuries ago, but is now one of the most popular dishes from the beautiful valleys of Kashmir in northern India.

PREPARATION: 15–20 mins plus marinating overnight or minimum of 2 hours
COOKING: 1½–2 hours
SERVES: 2–4 people

ROGHAN GOSHT

Ingredients

750g/1½lb boneless lamb, cut into 2.5cm/1in cubes
juice of 1 lemon
2 teaspoons salt
150ml/¼ pint natural yoghurt
4 tablespoons sunflower oil
1 onion, thinly sliced

BOWL 1
2.5cm/1in piece fresh ginger, peeled and grated or finely chopped
3 cloves garlic, crushed

BOWL 2
2 teaspoons ground cumin
2 teaspoons paprika
½ teaspoon freshly ground black pepper

BOWL 3
2 tablespoons tomato purée
½ teaspoon salt

The Day Before

- Place the lamb in a large dish and sprinkle with the lemon juice and salt, rubbing it in and mixing well. Stir in the yoghurt, cover with clingfilm and leave to marinate overnight in the fridge.

To Cook

1 Heat the oil in a large saucepan and fry the onion for 5 minutes until tender and translucent.
2 Add **BOWL 1** and continue frying for about 5 minutes until the onion is golden brown and slightly caramelised.
3 Lift the meat out of the marinade and add to the pan. Fry for about 5 minutes, turning regularly, until evenly browned and sealed on all sides.
4 Add **BOWL 2** and fry for 2–4 minutes, stirring occasionally to ensure that the meat is evenly coated.
5 Add the leftover marinade to the pan with **BOWL 3** and mix well. Cover and simmer gently for 1–1½ hours until the meat is tender.
6 Check and stir the meat every 20 minutes during cooking. Adjust the seasoning if necessary.

COOK'S TIPS Use lean meat or trim off any excessive fat or, for an even more authentic taste, cook with meat on the bone. Add a little water if the spice mixture gets too dry during cooking, and use Greek yoghurt for an even creamier taste.
SERVING SUGGESTIONS Serve with boiled basmati rice or chapattis (page 42) and a vegetable of your choice.

Lamb Passanda

Passanda dishes are becoming more and more popular. This lamb passanda gets a bit of a twist at the end by the use of fresh coconut to create a special sauce that is really succulent and delicious.

PREPARATION: 20–30 mins
COOKING: 1½–2 hours
SERVES: 4–6 people

MESH PASSANDA

Ingredients

4 tablespoons olive oil
450g/1lb lean lamb, cut into small cubes
2 potatoes, peeled and cut into 2.5cm/1in chunks
handful coriander leaves

BOWL 1
1 teaspoon cumin
4 cardamom pods
4 cloves
5cm/2in cinnamon stick
2 large onions, thinly sliced

BOWL 2
5cm/2in piece fresh ginger, peeled and minced
4 cloves garlic, crushed
½ teaspoon turmeric
1 teaspoon salt
½ teaspoon chilli powder

BOWL 3
½ fresh coconut, brown skin removed and flesh grated
2 teaspoons sugar
600ml/1 pint natural yoghurt

To Cook

1 Heat the oil in a large saucepan, add **BOWL 1** and fry for 3–4 minutes until the onions are soft and turning golden brown.

2 Add **BOWL 2**, stir well and fry gently for 2–3 minutes.

3 Add the lamb and simmer gently for 45 minutes until the lamb is almost ready but still not fully cooked. Add a little water if it gets too dry.

4 Place **BOWL 3** in a blender with 300ml (½ pint) water and process until smooth, then add to the pan with the potatoes and cook for another 35–40 minutes until the lamb is tender.

5 Adjust the seasoning if necessary and garnish with coriander.

COOK'S TIPS When cooking the lamb, put the pan on a low long simmer and add water if it gets too dry. You could use a pressure cooker to cook the lamb quickly.

SERVING SUGGESTION Serve with boiled basmati rice and a vegetable of your choice.

Lamb Korma

In India, mutton might be goat meat, not just sheep meat. Similarly, kid is often described as lamb. This dish involves cooking the meat with only a few spices in water, then mixing it with fried spices and all the juices from the meat to create a natural and very wholesome meat stock.

PREPARATION: 10–20 mins
COOKING: 2–2 1/4 hours
SERVES: 4–6 people

MESH KORMA

Ingredients

750g/1 1/2lb boneless lamb or mutton, cut into 2.5cm/1in cubes

4 tablespoons sunflower oil

1 green chilli, finely sliced

1/2 teaspoon saffron strands, steeped in 1 tablespoon hot water (optional)

BOWL 1

4 cloves

6 black peppercorns

two 5cm/2in cinnamon sticks

1 teaspoon cumin seeds

2 cardamom pods

BOWL 2

2 medium onions, finely chopped

4 cloves garlic, crushed

2.5cm/1in piece fresh ginger, peeled and grated

4 bay leaves

BOWL 3

1 teaspoon turmeric

1 teaspoon garam masala

1 teaspoon chilli powder

BOWL 4

300ml/1/2 pint natural yoghurt

1 1/2 teaspoons salt

To Cook

1 Place the lamb in a large saucepan with 600ml/1 pint water and **BOWL 1**. Bring to the boil, then reduce the heat, cover and simmer for 1 1/2 hours until the lamb is tender and the liquid has reduced by about half.

2 Heat the oil in another large saucepan, add **BOWL 2** and fry for 3–4 minutes until the onions are golden brown.

3 Add **BOWL 3**, mix well and cook gently for 5 minutes, stirring continuously so that the spices do not stick to the pan or burn.

4 Add **BOWL 4** and cook for another 5 minutes, stirring regularly.

5 Stir in the cooked lamb and all its juices, then simmer over a low heat for 10–15 minutes.

6 Transfer to a warm serving dish and scatter with the sliced green chilli and steeped saffron.

SERVING SUGGESTION Serve with basmati rice and vegetables.

Lamb Curry

Lamb curry is not just a popular restaurant dish but is also one of those curries many Indians like to make at home. It uses a variety of spices, cooked in a special way, to create a great taste.

PREPARATION: 30 mins
COOKING: 2 hours
SERVES: 4–6 people

MESH TARKARI

Ingredients

6 tablespoons sunflower oil
750g/1½lb boneless lamb, cut into 2.5cm/1in cubes
5 tomatoes, skinned and sliced
1½ teaspoons salt
1 teaspoon garam masala

BOWL 1

6 cloves
6 black peppercorns
1 teaspoon cumin seeds
5cm/2in cinnamon stick
2 cardamom pods

BOWL 2

1 large onion, finely sliced
4 bay leaves

BOWL 3

1 medium onion, chopped
6 cloves garlic, crushed
2.5cm/1in piece fresh ginger, peeled and chopped
1 tablespoon coriander seeds
1 teaspoon chilli powder
1 teaspoon turmeric

BOWL 4

150ml/¼ pint natural yoghurt
2 tablespoons tomato purée

To Cook

1 Heat 2 tablespoons of the oil in a large saucepan, add the lamb and **BOWL 1**. Fry for 10 minutes, stirring continuously to seal and brown the meat all over. Lift out the meat with a slotted spoon and set aside.

2 Add the remaining oil to the same pan with **BOWL 2** and fry for 5 minutes until the onion is golden brown.

3 Place **BOWL 3** in a blender with 4 tablespoons water and process until smooth. Add to the pan and fry for 1–2 minutes, stirring continuously.

4 Add **BOWL 4** and four of the tomatoes, mix well and cook for 10 minutes, stirring continuously.

5 Return the meat to the pan and simmer gently for 5–6 minutes.

6 Add the salt and 600ml/1 pint water and stir well. Bring to the boil, reduce the heat and simmer, covered, for 1–1½ hours until the meat is tender, stirring occasionally.

7 Add the garam masala, stir well and cook for 1–2 minutes.

8 Garnish with the remaining slices of tomato.

COOK'S TIPS Use meat on the bone for an even tastier, more authentic dish. Replace the water with beef stock for an even meatier taste.
SERVING SUGGESTIONS Serve with rice or naan bread (page 44) and a cucumber and tomato salad (page 32).

Dry-fried Meat Curry
Bhuna or bhoona means fried in Hindustani and is the term used for the process of cooking a spice paste in hot oil. This is a key part of the recipe because it removes the raw taste of the spices and creates the final, well-rounded taste of the dish. You can make this curry with any meat.

PREPARATION: 15–20 mins
COOKING: 1 hour
SERVES: 4–6 people

BHUNA GOSHT

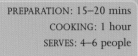

Ingredients

4 tablespoons sunflower oil
750g/1½lb lean beef or lamb, trimmed of excess fat and cut into 2.5cm/1in cubes

BOWL 1
2 medium onions, finely chopped
2 cloves garlic, crushed
2 tomatoes, skinned and chopped
1 tablespoon malt vinegar

BOWL 2
½ teaspoon chilli powder
½ teaspoon turmeric
1 teaspoon ground coriander
1 teaspoon garam masala

BOWL 3
50g/2oz creamed coconut
1½ teaspoons salt

To Cook

1 Heat 2 tablespoons of the oil in a large saucepan and fry the meat for 5–10 minutes, turning frequently, until browned and sealed all over.
2 Put **BOWL 1** in a blender and process to make a smooth onion paste.
3 In a separate saucepan, heat the remaining oil and fry the onion paste for 1 minute, stirring frequently.
4 Add **BOWL 2** and fry for 3–4 minutes, stirring continuously.
5 Add the meat and **BOWL 3**, stir well, cover and simmer for about 40 minutes until the meat is tender, stirring occasionally.

COOK'S TIPS This is a dry curry with very little gravy. If it gets too dry while cooking, add a little water and make sure you stir it frequently. Try it with different meat, such as braising steak or even lean pork. If you use chicken, this recipe will be even quicker to cook.
SERVING SUGGESTION Serve with chapattis (page 42) and a vegetable curry.

Minced Meat with Peas
Every Indian household probably has its own version of this recipe. This one is mild and simple, ideal for serving to children with rice. You could also use it as the meat mixture in a spicy shepherd's pie. It is very versatile and quick to make.

PREPARATION: 10–15 mins plus
1 hour marinating
COOKING: 40 minutes
SERVES: 4 people

KEEMA

Ingredients

750g/1½lb lean minced beef or lamb
2 tablespoons sunflower oil
2 medium tomatoes, coarsely chopped
450g/1lb frozen peas

BOWL 1
1 teaspoon salt
1 teaspoon freshly ground black pepper
juice of 1 lemon

BOWL 2
1 large onion, chopped
2 cloves garlic, crushed

BOWL 3
1 teaspoon ground ginger
1 teaspoon ground cumin
1 teaspoon ground coriander
1 teaspoon turmeric
2 teaspoons garam masala

To Cook

1 Place the minced meat in a large dish, add **BOWL 1** and mix well. Cover and leave to marinate for 1 hour.

2 Heat the oil in a large saucepan, add **BOWL 2** and fry for 2–3 minutes, stirring occasionally, until the onion is golden.

3 Add **BOWL 3** and continue frying for 2 minutes, stirring well.

4 Add the minced meat and fry gently for about 5 minutes, stirring well, until the meat is browned all over.

5 Stir in the tomatoes, cover and simmer gently for 20 minutes.

6 Mix in the peas, stir well and cook for 20–30 minutes. Adjust the seasoning if necessary.

COOK'S TIPS Use minced steak for a leaner dish. Try frozen or canned sweetcorn as a delicious alternative to peas. This recipe is perfect as a meat filling for samosas (page 21).
SERVING SUGGESTIONS Serve with rice and lentils (pages 34 and 113) or simply with chapattis (page 42) or naan bread (page 44).

Calcutta Beef Curry

This curry is one of the most famous dishes from the Bengal region of India. Its origins are probably rooted in Muslim and Christian cultures, as Hindus do not eat beef. Bengal is known for its fusion of different races and religions and has a wonderfully exciting mixed cuisine. The freshly crushed spices give this dish an extra zest that will delight your tastebuds.

CALCUTTA GOSHT

PREPARATION: 20–25 mins
COOKING: 1–1¼ hours
SERVES: 4 people

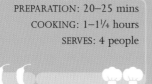

Ingredients

4 tablespoons sunflower oil
450g/1lb braising steak, trimmed of excess fat and cut into 1x4cm/½x1½in strips
300ml/½ pint well-seasoned beef stock

BOWL 1
1 medium onion, thinly sliced
2 cloves garlic, crushed

BOWL 2
1 teaspoon cumin seeds
3 teaspoons coriander seeds
1 teaspoon black peppercorns
1 teaspoon crushed red chillies

BOWL 3
2.5cm/1in piece fresh ginger, peeled and grated or finely chopped
1 teaspoon turmeric

BOWL 4
100g/4oz creamed coconut, dissolved in 300ml/½ pint hot water
juice of 1 lemon

To Cook

1 Heat the oil in a large saucepan, add **BOWL 1** and fry for 3–5 minutes until the onion is golden brown.
2 Crush **BOWL 2** using a pestle and mortar and add to the pan. Fry for 2 minutes, stirring continuously to blend with the onion mixture.
3 Add **BOWL 3** and fry for another minute, stirring well.
4 Add the beef and stir well to coat with the spices. Fry for another 5 minutes, stirring well to seal the meat on all sides.
5 Pour in the stock, bring to the boil, then reduce the heat, cover and simmer for 10–15 minutes.
6 Pour in **BOWL 4** and stir well. Cover and simmer gently for 40 minutes until the meat is beautifully tender, stirring occasionally.

COOK'S TIPS When you pound the spices with the pestle and mortar, break them up but don't reduce them to powder. If the curry has too much liquid, rapidly boil off any excess to thicken the gravy.
SERVING SUGGESTION Serve with boiled rice and a vegetable curry of your choice.

Beef with Onions

It is commonly known among Indian chefs that you need to use as much onion as the dish requires and then a little more to get the right dopeyaja taste. This recipe is very hot.

PREPARATION: 20–30 mins
COOKING: 1¼–1½ hours
SERVES: 5–6 people

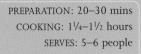

GOSHT DOPEYAJA

Ingredients

4 tablespoons sunflower oil
750g/1½lb braising steak, trimmed of excess fat and cut into 2.5cm/1in cubes
3 large onions, thickly sliced
900ml/1½ pints beef stock

BOWL 1

1 teaspoon ground coriander
1 teaspoon turmeric
1 teaspoon freshly ground black pepper
2 teaspoons ground cumin
2 teaspoons chilli powder
5cm/2in cinnamon stick

BOWL 2

3 large onions, coarsely chopped
4 green chillies, trimmed
2 cloves garlic, crushed
5cm/2in piece fresh ginger, peeled and grated or finely chopped
juice of 1 lemon

BOWL 3

3 teaspoons garam masala
1 teaspoon salt
juice of 1 lemon

To Cook

1 Heat the oil in a large saucepan and fry the beef for 5 minutes, turning frequently until browned and sealed on all sides. Lift out the beef using a slotted spoon and set aside.

2 Reheat the oil in the pan and fry the onions for 5 minutes until golden brown.

3 Add **BOWL 1** and fry briskly for 1–2 minutes.

4 Return the beef to the pan and stir well to coat in the spice mixture.

5 Add the beef stock and bring to the boil. Reduce the heat, cover and simmer gently for 10 minutes.

6 Put **BOWL 2** in a blender and process until smooth, then add to the pan. Stir well, cover and cook for 40–45 minutes until the beef is becoming tender.

7 Add **BOWL 3**, stir and cook for another 10 minutes until the beef is completely tender. Adjust the seasoning if necessary.

COOK'S TIPS The beef should be in a fairly thick gravy. If necessary, boil off any excess liquid at the end of the cooking. Reduce the heat of this dish by using fewer green chillies.

SERVING SUGGESTIONS This dish is very hot, so serve it with rice, raita to cool down (page 38) and a milder vegetable curry such as spinach with potato (page 112) or roasted aubergine (page 124).

Beef in Yoghurt
This hot dish originates from the north of India where the use of yoghurt is typical to the cuisine.

PREPARATION: 25–35 mins plus marinating overnight or minimum of 8 hours
COOKING: 1–1¼ mins
SERVES: 5–6 people

DAHI GOSHT

Ingredients

1kg/2lb braising steak, trimmed of excess fat and cut into 1cm/½in slices
4 tablespoons sunflower oil
2 large onions, thinly sliced
4 green chillies, trimmed and sliced
150ml/¼ pint beef stock

BOWL 1
300ml/1 pint natural yoghurt
4 cloves garlic, crushed
1 teaspoon coriander seeds
2 teaspoons chilli powder
2 teaspoons ground cumin
2 teaspoons freshly ground black pepper
2 teaspoons salt

BOWL 2
5cm/2in piece fresh ginger, peeled and grated or finely chopped
4 cloves
4 cardamom pods

BOWL 3
50g/2oz desiccated coconut
50g/2oz ground almonds

The Day Before

• Put **BOWL 1** in a blender and process until smooth. Pour over the sliced beef, cover and leave to marinate overnight in the fridge.

To Cook

1 Heat the oil in a large saucepan and fry the onions for 4–6 minutes, stirring continuously, until caramelised and golden.
2 Add **BOWL 2** and fry for 2 minutes, stirring well.
3 Stir in the beef and marinade, turn up the heat and cook for 5–10 minutes until the beef changes colour, stirring frequently.
4 Add the green chillies, stirring well, and cook for 1 minute.
5 Pour in the stock and bring to the boil, then reduce the heat and simmer for 30 minutes.
6 Stir in **BOWL 3** and simmer for 15 minutes until the beef is completely tender. Adjust the seasoning if necessary.

COOK'S TIPS Use fewer green chillies to reduce the heat. Add 1–2 tablespoons malt vinegar or water to the ingredients in the liquidiser if the marinade looks too dry and thick.
SERVING SUGGESTION Serve with plain boiled basmati rice and a vegetable curry of your choice, with raita (page 38) and a cucumber and tomato salad (page 32) to help cool the palate.

Beef Curry with Tomatoes

The tomatoes in this Muslim dish give the beef a special flavour, and together they produce a very fragrant smell. The tomatoes also add to the colour. It's very easy to cook.

PREPARATION: 15–20 mins
COOKING: 1½–2 hours
SERVES: 4–6 people

GARUR GOSHT TARKARI

Ingredients

3 tablespoons sunflower oil
450g/1lb braising steak, cut into 2.5cm/1in cubes
400g/14oz tin chopped tomatoes
1 teaspoon salt

BOWL 1

1 medium onion, finely chopped
2 cloves garlic, crushed

BOWL 2

½ teaspoon ground ginger
½ teaspoon ground cumin
1 teaspoon turmeric
1 teaspoon ground coriander
1 teaspoon chilli powder
1 teaspoon freshly ground black pepper

BOWL 3

3 cloves
3 cardamom pods
2.5cm/1in cinnamon stick

BOWL 4

150ml/¼ pint natural yoghurt
1 tablespoon malt vinegar

To Cook

1 Heat the oil in a saucepan, add the beef and fry for 4–5 minutes, turning to seal on all sides. Lift the meat out of the pan and set aside.

2 Reheat the oil in the pan, add **BOWL 1** and fry for about 5 minutes until the onion is golden brown.

3 Stir in **BOWL 2** and fry for 2 minutes, stirring frequently.

4 Add **BOWL 3** and stir over moderate heat for another minute.

5 Return the beef to the pan with the tomatoes and salt, bring to the boil and stir well.

6 Stir in **BOWL 4** and bring to the boil. Reduce the heat, cover and simmer gently for 1–1½ hours until the beef is tender, stirring occasionally. Adjust the seasoning if necessary.

COOK'S TIPS Use Greek yoghurt for a creamier sauce or low-fat natural yoghurt for a leaner dish.

SERVING SUGGESTIONS Serve with basmati rice and spinach and potato (page 112) or, for a hotter flavour, fried ladies fingers (page 121).

Beef Madras
This is a bold curry from the city of Madras on the eastern coast of southern India. Expect this one to be fairly hot.

PREPARATION: 30 mins plus
1 hour marinating
COOKING: 1½ hours
SERVES: 4–6 people

GOSHT MADRAS

Ingredients

450g/1lb braising steak, cut into 2.5cm/1in cubes
4 tablespoons sunflower oil
4 tablespoons tomato purée
300ml/½ pint beef stock
2 teaspoons garam masala

BOWL 1

2 teaspoons salt
juice of 1 lemon

BOWL 2

1 large onion, finely chopped
2 cloves garlic, crushed
2 dried red chillies, crumbled

BOWL 3

1 teaspoon ground ginger
1 teaspoon turmeric
1 teaspoon ground cumin
2 teaspoons ground coriander
2 teaspoons freshly ground black pepper

To Cook

1 Place the beef in a large dish, add **BOWL 1** and mix well. Cover and leave to marinate for 1 hour.

2 Heat the oil in a large, heavy-based saucepan, add **BOWL 2** and fry for 3 minutes until the onion is golden brown and caramelised.

3 Add **BOWL 3** and fry for 2–3 minutes, stirring frequently.

4 Add the beef, together with any remaining marinade, and fry for 5–10 minutes, turning the meat to brown and seal it on all sides.

5 Stir in the tomato purée and the beef stock and bring to the boil.

6 Reduce the heat, cover and simmer gently for 40 minutes, stirring occasionally, until the beef is very tender.

7 Sprinkle with the garam masala and cook for another 10 minutes. Adjust the seasoning if necessary.

COOK'S TIPS This is a hot curry with a thick gravy; boil off any excess liquid if it seems to be too runny. The longer you leave the meat to marinate, the better the taste.

SERVING SUGGESTIONS Serve piping hot with basmati rice and some milder vegetable curries, such as spinach and potato (page 112), or dry hot potato (page 125).

Baked Beef

This is an unusual but very practical and easy way of making a curry because it is cooked in an oven. This leaves you free to do other things or simply relax while it is cooking – what could be better?

JHALSANO GARUR GOSHT

PREPARATION: 30–40 mins plus marinating overnight
COOKING: 1–1³/4 hours
SERVES: 4 people

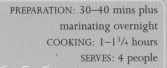

Ingredients

450g/1lb stewing steak, trimmed of excess fat and cut into 1cm/¹/₂in slices
2 large onions, sliced
4 tablespoons sesame oil

BOWL 1
juice of 2 lemons
2 teaspoons salt

BOWL 2
2 green chillies, trimmed and sliced
2 cloves garlic, crushed
2 teaspoons black peppercorns
5cm/2in cinnamon stick
6 cloves
6 cardamom pods
1 teaspoon ground ginger
1 teaspoon ground cumin
2 teaspoons turmeric
2 teaspoons ground coriander
2 teaspoons chilli powder

The Day Before

• Put the beef in a large dish, mix with **BOWL 1**, then cover and leave to marinate overnight in the fridge.

To Cook

1 Preheat the oven to 180°C/350°F/Gas Mark 4. Arrange half the sliced onions in the base of a large, ovenproof casserole dish and add the marinated meat mixture.

2 Heat the sesame oil in a large saucepan, add the remaining onion and fry for about 5 minutes until translucent.

3 Add **BOWL 2**, stir well and fry for 2–3 minutes.

4 Spread the fried spice and onion mixture over the beef in the casserole dish, cover and cook in the preheated oven for 1¹/2 hours until the beef is completely tender. Turn the meat over occasionally to make sure it doesn't become dry on top.

> **COOK'S TIPS** Use lamb instead of beef for a change of flavour.
> **SERVING SUGGESTIONS** Serve with basmati rice or naan bread (page 44) and a vegetable curry, such as spinach with potato (page 112) or pea and potato (page 114).

Lamb and Potato Curry
Although this particular recipe uses lamb, you can use any type of meat for this curry – lamb, beef or pork.

PREPARATION: 15–20 mins
COOKING: 1–1½ hours
SERVES: 6 people

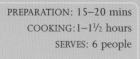

ALOO GOSHT

Ingredients

4 tablespoons sunflower oil
1kg/2lb lean boneless lamb, cut into 2.5cm/1in cubes
300ml/½ pint beef stock
450g/1lb potatoes, peeled and cut into 2.5cm/1in chunks

BOWL 1
1 large onion, sliced
2 cloves garlic, crushed
5cm/2in piece fresh ginger, peeled and grated or finely chopped

BOWL 2
2 teaspoons turmeric
1 teaspoon ground coriander
1 teaspoon ground cumin
1 teaspoon freshly ground black pepper
6 cloves
6 cardamom pods
2 teaspoons chilli powder

BOWL 3
2 tomatoes, coarsely chopped
3 teaspoons garam masala
1 teaspoon salt

To Cook

1 Heat the oil in a large saucepan, add **BOWL 1** and fry for 3 minutes until the onion is golden brown.

2 Add **BOWL 2** and stir fry for 1–2 minutes.

3 Add the meat, stir well to coat with the spice mixture and cook for 2–3 minutes. Keep stirring to seal the meat on all sides.

4 Pour in the stock and bring to the boil. Reduce the heat, cover and simmer gently for 30–40 minutes until the meat is almost cooked through.

5 Add the potato, stir well, cover and simmer for 15–20 minutes until the potato chunks are tender.

6 Add **BOWL 3**, stir well and cook for 5–10 minutes until the meat is tender and the potatoes soft.

COOK'S TIPS Cook this recipe using meat on the bone for an even tastier, more authentic dish. Waxy potatoes, such as Desirée, give the best results.
SERVING SUGGESTION Delicious with basmati rice, fried ladies fingers (page 121) and tomato chutney.

CHICKEN, TURKEY AND DUCK

3

Baked Whole Chicken
Tandoori chicken is a restaurant favourite. The Moguls, who invented the tandoor – a cylindrical clay oven that gives food a unique flavour – mastered this style of cooking, but you can re-create the taste using a large casserole dish and a hot oven.

PREPARATION: 20–30 mins plus
30 mins marinating
COOKING: 1–1¼ hour
SERVES: 4–6 people

TANDOORI MURGH

Ingredients

1.5kg/3lb chicken, skinned
4 tablespoons sunflower oil
½ teaspoon saffron strands
1 lemon, cut into wedges

BOWL 1

2 teaspoons turmeric
2 tablespoons coriander seeds
3 teaspoons garam masala
4 cloves garlic, crushed
4 large red chillies
1cm/½in piece fresh ginger, peeled and chopped
2 teaspoons paprika
1 teaspoon salt
juice of 2 lemons
1 large onion, chopped

To Cook

1 Place **BOWL 1** in a blender and process until smooth.
2 Put the chicken into the top of a steamer over boiling water and steam for 10–15 minutes to tenderise the flesh.
3 Transfer the chicken to a board and prick it all over with a fork, then rub in the blended mixture, inside and out, and leave to marinate for 30 minutes.
4 Heat the oil gently in a large saucepan over a low heat. Lift the chicken out of the marinade, place it in the pan with the saffron and cook gently for about 15 minutes, turning occasionally. Preheat the oven to 200°C/400°F/Gas Mark 6.
5 Transfer the chicken and the marinade to a large ovenproof casserole dish, cover with a tightly fitting lid and cook for 20–30 minutes until the chicken is tender. Garnish with lemon wedges.

COOK'S TIPS Use a knife to prick the chicken instead of a fork to get deeper cuts in which to rub the spice mixture.

Royal Chicken

Shahi murgh means chicken for kings. This dish might even have been made for a Persian king, as it uses cloves, cardamoms and almonds to give an aromatic and scented taste that is typically Persian. It's amazing what you can do with just a few spices and some fresh ingredients.

PREPARATION: 30–40 mins
COOKING: 1–1¼ hour
SERVES: 4–5 people

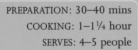

SHAHI MURGH

Ingredients

4 tablespoons sunflower oil
4–5 chicken legs, skinned
handful coriander leaves, coarsely chopped

BOWL 1
2 green chillies, chopped
1 large onion, chopped
1 clove garlic, crushed

BOWL 2
2.5cm/1in piece fresh ginger, peeled and sliced
10 cardamom pods
10 cloves

BOWL 3
1 teaspoon salt
1 teaspoon natural yoghurt
pinch of saffron strands
1 teaspoon paprika

BOWL 4
100g/4oz flaked blanched almonds
100g/4oz fresh coconut, grated

To Cook

1 Heat the oil in a large, heavy-based saucepan, add **BOWL 1** and fry gently for 1–2 minutes until the onion is golden brown.

2 Add **BOWL 2** and cook for another 2 minutes until sizzling.

3 Add the chicken and cook for about 12 minutes, turning to seal on all sides.

4 Mix in **BOWL 3** and simmer gently for another 35–40 minutes until the sauce has thickened.

5 Add **BOWL 4** and simmer for 10–15 minutes until the chicken is tender and falling away from the bone.

6 Adjust the seasoning if necessary and sprinkle with coriander.

> **COOK'S TIPS** The sauce should be thick. Boil it rapidly if necessary to evaporate any excess water. Crush the cardamom pods lightly to release more of the flavour. Saffron is expensive but it's worth splashing out here for the special flavour it gives. If you can't get fresh coconut, use creamed coconut. You should be able to get this in your local supermarket or ethnic deli.

Royal Turkey

This is an adaptation of a beef recipe, with a Christmas theme in mind. Use the dark leg meat of the turkey because it gives a better flavour. I've added dried prunes to give this dish an exotic sweet and sour taste, making it extra special.

PREPARATION: 20–30 mins
COOKING: 1¼–1½ hour
SERVES: 4–6 people

RAJ
PAHKI

Ingredients

2 teaspoons rice flour
4 tablespoons sunflower oil
750g/1½lb boneless turkey leg meat, cut into 1cm/½in strips
600ml/1 pint chicken stock
2 teaspoons garam masala

BOWL 1
juice of 2 lemons
1 tablespoon malt vinegar
2 tablespoons clear honey
4 cardamom pods
4 cloves

BOWL 2
1 small onion, sliced
2 cloves garlic, crushed

BOWL 3
2.5cm/1in piece fresh ginger, peeled and grated or finely chopped
1 teaspoon ground cumin
½ teaspoon freshly ground black pepper
2 teaspoons ground coriander
1 teaspoon salt
6 dried stoned prunes

To Cook

1 Transfer **BOWL 1** to a small saucepan, bring to the boil and simmer for 2–3 minutes. Remove from the heat.

2 Stir in the rice flour and mix well using a fork or whisk. You may get a few lumps but these will break up when you add the mixture to the main dish.

3 Return the mixture to the heat and whisk again for 1 minute to thicken the sauce, then set aside.

4 Heat the oil in a large saucepan with **BOWL 2** and cook for 5 minutes until the onion is golden brown.

5 Add the turkey strips and cook, stirring continuously, until sealed on all sides.

6 Add **BOWL 3**, pour in the stock, stir and bring to the boil.

7 Reduce the heat and simmer gently for 40–45 minutes.

8 Stir in the garam masala to the thickened sauce mixture and simmer for 15–20 minutes until the gravy is smooth and rich.

COOK'S TIPS Use the juice of 4 limes instead of 2 lemons for a sharper taste. Indian sweet and sour is very different from the Chinese version. The gravy is rich and liquid, more like an English stew, and not thick and glutinous at all. For a really authentic aroma, sprinkle with 1 tablespoon kewra water before serving. You can get this at your local supermarket or specialist Indian grocer.

Hyderabad Chicken Curry
This recipe from Hyderabad in central India uses lots of fresh coconut, which is typical of central/southern Indian cuisine. Everywhere you travel you will find regional dishes that reflect the special character of the area, and this dish is a good example.

PREPARATION: 15–20 mins
COOKING: 1–1¼ hours
SERVES: 5–6 people

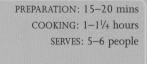

HYDERABADI TARKARI

Ingredients

4 tablespoons sunflower oil
5–6 chicken thighs and 5–6 drumsticks, skinned
300ml/½ pint chicken stock
4 tablespoons tomato purée
juice of 1 lemon
1 teaspoon garam masala
handful chopped coriander leaves

BOWL 1
1 medium onion, sliced
2 cloves garlic, crushed

BOWL 2
6 cloves
6 cardamom pods
½ teaspoon ground aniseed
5cm/2in cinnamon stick
1 teaspoon ground cumin
2 teaspoons turmeric
2 teaspoons freshly ground black pepper
2 teaspoons chilli powder
2 teaspoons ground coriander
2.5cm/1in piece fresh ginger, peeled and grated

BOWL 3
½ fresh coconut, flesh removed and finely shaved,
or 2 tablespoons desiccated coconut
1 teaspoon salt

To Cook

1 Heat the oil in a frying pan, add **BOWL 1** and fry for 5–10 minutes until the onion is soft and golden brown.
2 Add **BOWL 2**, stir well and fry for 1–2 minutes to cook the spices.
3 Reduce the heat, add the chicken, stock and tomato purée and bring to the boil.
4 Add **BOWL 3** and mix well. Reduce the heat, cover and simmer gently for 40–60 minutes, stirring occasionally, until the chicken is tender and falls away from the bone.
5 Add the lemon juice and garam masala and simmer for another 3–4 minutes.
6 Adjust the seasoning if necessary and garnish with coriander.

COOK'S TIPS If you prefer you can just use 10–12 chicken thighs.
SERVING SUGGESTIONS Serve with rice and a vegetable curry of your choice. I particularly like this dish served with pea and potato curry (page 114).

Delhi Chicken Curry
This chicken dish is typical of the Delhi area. What singles this recipe out is the sweet and sour taste produced by the tomato purée and lemon juice, and the large quantity of fresh ginger. It creates a tantalisingly exotic yet mild flavour that people love.

PREPARATION: 15–20 mins
COOKING: 1–1¼ hours
SERVES: 4–6 people

DELHI MURGH TARKARI

Ingredients

4 tablespoons sunflower oil
5–6 chicken thighs and 5–6 drumsticks, skinned
300ml/½ pint chicken stock

BOWL 1
1 large onion, sliced
2 cloves garlic, crushed

BOWL 2
4 cloves
4 cardamom pods
2.5cm/1in cinnamon stick
two 5cm/2in pieces fresh ginger, peeled and sliced

BOWL 3
1 teaspoon chilli powder
2 teaspoons ground coriander
½ teaspoon turmeric
2 teaspoons ground cumin

BOWL 4
juice of 2 lemons
4 tablespoons tomato purée

BOWL 5
1 tablespoon chopped coriander leaves
2 teaspoons salt
1 teaspoon freshly ground black pepper

To Cook

1 Heat the oil in a large, heavy-based saucepan and fry the chicken pieces until opaque white and sealed all over. Remove the chicken from the pan and set aside.

2 Reheat the oil in the pan, add **BOWL 1** and fry for 5 minutes until the onion is golden brown and caramelised.

3 Add **BOWL 2** and fry for 2–4 minutes, stirring occasionally.

4 Mix in **BOWL 3** and cook for another 2 minutes, stirring continuously so that the spices do not stick to the pan or burn.

5 Add **BOWL 4** and stir well to make a smooth sauce, then add the chicken pieces and stock. Stir well to coat the chicken all over, then bring to the boil.

6 Reduce the heat and simmer gently for 35–50 minutes until the chicken is tender and falls away from the bone.

7 Stir in **BOWL 5**, mix well and heat for 1–2 minutes to blend the flavours.

COOK'S TIPS Use 10–12 chicken thighs instead of drumsticks, if you prefer. This dish is excellent for freezing to use at a later date.

Duck Curry

As a child, I remember my grandmother keeping lovely white ducks. I could never understand why they would disappear every now and then … obviously they went into making this duck curry!

HASHER TARKARI

PREPARATION: 20–30 mins plus
2 hours marinating
COOKING: 1½–2 hours
SERVES: 5–6 people

Ingredients

750g/1½lb duck breasts or portions, skinned and cut into 4cm/1½in cubes
3 tablespoons sunflower oil
1 onion, thinly sliced
handful chopped coriander leaves

BOWL 1

juice of 2 limes
1 teaspoon salt

BOWL 2

1 onion, roughly chopped
1 teaspoon chilli powder
1 teaspoon turmeric
2 teaspoons paprika
4 tablespoons natural yoghurt
2 cloves garlic, crushed
1cm/½in piece fresh ginger, peeled and chopped

BOWL 3

1 teaspoon black peppercorns, lightly crushed
4 green chillies, sliced lengthways

BOWL 4

6 tomatoes, cut into quarters
2 teaspoons garam masala

To Cook

1 Add **BOWL 1** to the duck in a large dish, mix well and set aside to marinate for about 2 hours.

2 Heat the oil in a large saucepan and add the onion. Fry for about 5 minutes until golden brown and lightly caramelised.

3 Transfer **BOWL 2** to a blender and process until smooth. Add to the pan, stir well and cook for 2–3 minutes.

4 Add **BOWL 3**, mix well and cook for another 1–2 minutes.

5 Stir in 150ml/¼ pint water and bring to the boil. Add the duck, mix well and simmer, covered, for 1–1½ hours.

6 Add **BOWL 4** and cook for another 10–20 minutes until the duck is cooked and tender. Stir in the coriander.

Aromatic Roast Chicken
This recipe uses aromatics such as cardamom and saffron rather than bold spices to achieve a delicate fragrance and flavour. The dish also involves the use of a masala (spicy sauce) to coat the chicken the night before – a bit like a marinade but a lot drier.

PREPARATION: 30 mins plus marinating overnight
COOKING: 1¼–1½ hours
SERVES: 4 people

SHUGANDHA MURGH

Ingredients

1.5kg/3lb chicken
1 teaspoon salt
3 tablespoons sunflower oil
1 medium onion, peeled and finely chopped

BOWL 1
150ml/¼ pint natural yoghurt
2 cloves garlic, peeled and finely chopped
5cm/2in piece fresh ginger, peeled and finely chopped
seed from 15 cardamom pods
1 teaspoon cumin seeds
1 teaspoon chilli powder

BOWL 2
5cm/2in cinnamon stick, broken into small pieces
6 cloves

BOWL 3
pinch of saffron strands, just covered with boiling water

The Day Before

• Put **BOWL 1** in a blender for 1 minute. Place the chicken in a roasting dish and rub with the salt. Set aside for 10 minutes. Take the masala from the blender and spread it all over the chicken, rubbing it in well. Cover the bird and put it in the fridge, leaving the masala to penetrate and flavour the flesh overnight.

To Cook

1 Heat the oil in a saucepan and fry the onion for 4–5 minutes until soft.
2 Add **BOWL 2** and cook for another 5 minutes, stirring occasionally.
3 Remove from the heat and spoon this mixture into the cavity of the chicken (a bit like stuffing).
4 Pour **BOWL 3** over the chicken.
5 Preheat the oven to 180°C/350°F/Gas Mark 4. Cover the bird tightly with foil and roast for about 45 minutes.
6 Remove the foil and continue to cook the chicken for 15–20 minutes, allowing it to brown nicely.

COOK'S TIPS To check whether the chicken is cooked, prick the breast or leg with a sharp knife. If the juices run clear, the meat is cooked.
SERVING SUGGESTION Serve with vegetables of your choice.

Chicken with Lentils

This is a popular recipe in restaurants but can easily be cooked at home at your leisure. This recipe can be traced back to its Parsee origins, for whom dhansak is a special dish.

PREPARATION: 20–30 mins plus soaking overnight
COOKING: 1½–1¾ hours
SERVES: 5–6 people

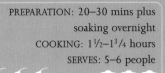

MURGH DHANSAK

Ingredients

225g/8oz lentils (half red and half green), rinsed and soaked overnight in plenty of water

5-6 chicken thighs and 5-6 drumsticks, skinned

3 tablespoons sunflower oil

2 handfuls coriander, coarsely chopped

BOWL 1

1 large onion, chopped

225g/8oz aubergine, cut into 2.5cm/1in cubes

450g/1lb potatoes, peeled and cut into

2.5cm/1in pieces

225g/8oz spinach leaves, coarsely chopped

BOWL 2

1 large onion, thinly sliced

6 green chillies, stems removed

BOWL 3

2 large onions, thinly sliced

3 cloves garlic, crushed

5cm/2in piece fresh ginger, peeled and finely chopped

BOWL 4

3 bay leaves

8 cloves

8 cardamom pods

5cm/2in cinnamon stick

½ teaspoon mustard seeds

2 teaspoons turmeric

2 teaspoons ground cumin

1 teaspoon coriander seeds

½ teaspoon ground fenugreek

2 teaspoons black pepper & 1 teaspoon salt

To Cook

1 Drain the lentils and place them in a large saucepan with the chicken. Add 600ml/1 pint water with **BOWL 1** and, heating very slowly, simmer for 5–10 minutes until the potatoes begin to soften.

2 Lift out the chicken pieces using a slotted spoon and set aside.

3 Turn up the heat and bring the lentil mixture to simmering point. Cook for 30–40 minutes until the lentils have completely broken up.

4 Pour the lentil mixture into a blender, add **BOWL 2** and process to make a smooth, thick sauce. Set aside.

5 Heat the oil in a large saucepan, add **BOWL 3** and sizzle for 2–3 minutes until the onion is golden brown.

6 Add **BOWL 4** and fry for another 3–4 minutes to cook the spices.

7 Pour in the lentil sauce from the blender and bring to the boil, stirring gently.

8 Reduce the heat and add the chicken pieces, then simmer gently for 20–25 minutes until the chicken is cooked and falls away from the bone.

9 Adjust the seasoning if necessary and stir in the coriander.

COOK'S TIPS Use 10–12 chicken thighs instead of drumsticks or joint a whole chicken into 10–12 pieces. You can use frozen leaf spinach if you are unable to get fresh.

SERVING SUGGESTION Serve with basmati rice and spinach with potato (page 112).

Hot Chicken Madras
For those who like it hot, this recipe uses a subtle combination of spices to produce a hot and spicy but delicate flavour.

PREPARATION: 20 mins plus
2 hours marinating
COOKING: 1¼–1½ hours
SERVES: 5–6 people

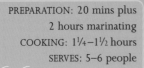

MADRASI MURGH

Ingredients

5–6 chicken thighs and 5–6 drumsticks, skinned
4 tablespoons sunflower oil
1 green chilli, split lengthways
2 bay leaves
2 teaspoons garam masala

BOWL 1
juice of 1 lemon
2 teaspoons chilli powder
2 teaspoons freshly ground black pepper
1 teaspoon salt

BOWL 2
2 large onions, sliced
3 cloves garlic, crushed
5cm/2in piece fresh ginger, peeled and grated
or finely chopped

BOWL 3
4 teaspoons ground cumin
2 teaspoons ground coriander
½ teaspoon turmeric

To Cook

1 Make a couple of cuts across the flesh of each chicken leg using a sharp knife. Place the chicken in a dish with **BOWL 1**. Mix well and set aside to marinate for 2 hours.

2 Heat the oil in a large saucepan, add **BOWL 2** and cook for 3 minutes until the onion is golden brown.

3 Add **BOWL 3** and cook for another 2 minutes, stirring well.

4 Mix in the green chilli and chicken pieces, together with the marinade, and fry for 5–10 minutes until the chicken is sealed and golden all over.

5 Add the bay leaves and 900ml/1½ pints boiling water and bring to the boil. Reduce the heat, cover and simmer gently for 35–40 minutes.

6 Add the garam masala and stir well. Cook for another 10 minutes until the chicken is tender and falls away from the bone. Adjust the seasoning if necessary.

Chicken with Yoghurt

This is a mild, dry dish from northern India that uses several cooking techniques: marinating, frying and poaching. It also reflects the northern Indian style of cooking in the subtle use of spices to bring out the flavour of the meat rather than masking it with overpowering heat.

PREPARATION: 30 mins plus marinating overnight or minimum of 2 hours
COOKING: 1 hour
SERVES: 4–6 people

DAHI MURGH

Ingredients

4–6 chicken thighs and 4–6 drumsticks, skinned
1 large green pepper, de-seeded and coarsely chopped
2 tablespoons sunflower oil
small handful coriander leaves, coarsely chopped

BOWL 1

4 green chillies, coarsely chopped
4 cloves garlic, chopped
7.5cm/3in piece fresh ginger, peeled and coarsely chopped
600ml/1 pint natural yoghurt
1 teaspoon paprika
1 teaspoon salt

BOWL 2

½ teaspoon freshly ground black pepper
1 teaspoon sugar

The Day Before

• Make several cuts across the flesh of each piece of chicken using a sharp knife and set aside. Pour **BOWL 1** into a blender and process until smooth. Add the green pepper and process again until well broken up. Pour the mixture over the chicken, cover and leave to marinate overnight in the fridge.

To Cook

1 Heat the oil in a heavy-based saucepan, lift the chicken pieces from the marinade (setting this aside), drain thoroughly and fry briskly for 1–2 minutes until sealed all over.
2 Add the reserved marinade and **BOWL 2** to the pan and continue to cook over a moderate heat for 10 minutes, stirring occasionally to keep the chicken coated with the sauce.
3 Cover and cook over a reduced heat for about 30 minutes, turning every 10 minutes, until the sauce has almost disappeared and the chicken is tender and falling away from the bone.
4 Adjust the seasoning if necessary and stir in the coriander.

COOK'S TIPS Use low-fat natural yoghurt if you want to reduce the calorie content. It's more traditional to cook this recipe using a whole chicken, but I think it's easier to use chicken pieces.
SERVING SUGGESTIONS This dry curry is delicious with chapattis (page 42) or naan bread (page 44) and some vegetables.

Chicken Korma

With spectacular mountains, magnificent waterfalls and valleys of emerald green, the beautiful borderlands of Pakistan and Kashmir are a cultural tapestry of Mongolian, Turkish and Persian influences. This area is also home to the korma style of cooking, with its creamy textures and subtle blend of spices.

PREPARATION: 30 mins plus marinating overnight or minimum of 2 hours
COOKING: 1–1½ hours
SERVES: 4 people

MURGH KORMA

Ingredients

4 chicken thighs and 4 drumsticks, skinned
3 tablespoons olive oil
1 large onion, thinly sliced
large handful chopped coriander

BOWL 1
600ml/1 pint natural yoghurt
2.5cm/1in piece fresh ginger, peeled and grated or finely chopped
75g/3oz sultanas
4 cloves garlic, crushed
1 teaspoon sugar
½ teaspoon salt

BOWL 2
5 bay leaves
6 cloves
6 cardamom pods
5cm/2in cinnamon stick

The Day Before

• Mix **BOWL 1** thoroughly and pour over the chicken in a large dish. Turn the chicken to coat all the pieces, then cover and leave to marinate overnight in the fridge.

To Cook

1 Heat the oil in a large saucepan, add the onion and fry for 2–3 minutes until translucent.
2 Add **BOWL 2** and continue to fry for 5–10 minutes until the onion is brown and lightly caramelised.
3 Reserving the marinade, lift out the chicken pieces and add to the pan. Fry briskly for 5–10 minutes until golden and sealed all over.
4 Mix in the reserved korma marinade and bring to the boil. Cover and simmer for 40–60 minutes, stirring occasionally, until the chicken is tender.
5 Garnish with coriander.

COOK'S TIPS Don't worry if the yoghurt separates when heated – this is all part of the cooking process. If the chicken sticks to the bottom of the saucepan, this is fine. When you add the korma marinade, stir well. This will remove the stickiness and help blend the bits into the sauce to give the dish extra flavour.

Chicken Vindaloo
This is a classic dish from Goa with a surprising history. It started as a Portuguese dish with vinegar and garlic. The Goans added their own blend of spices and chilli to the garlic and vinegar to make a spicy cooking paste called vindaloo masala. The end result is a delightfully subtle yet hot and spicy taste.

PREPARATION: 30 mins
COOKING: 1 hour
SERVES: 4 people

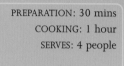

MURGH VINDALOO

Ingredients

4–6 tablespoons sunflower oil

4 chicken thighs and 4 drumsticks, skinned

2 medium onions, finely chopped

300ml/½ pint chicken stock

BOWL 1

4 cloves garlic, crushed

2 red chillies, finely sliced

3 tablespoons malt vinegar

juice of 1 lemon

1 teaspoon salt

1 teaspoon sugar

3 teaspoons ground coriander

2 teaspoons ground cumin

½ teaspoon ground cardamom

2 teaspoons turmeric

½ teaspoon ground cloves

1 teaspoon freshly ground black pepper

BOWL 2

2 teaspoons garam masala

4 bay leaves

2 dried chillies

(optional) **BOWL 3**

1 teaspoon freshly ground black pepper

2 teaspoons crushed dried red chillies

3 teaspoons chilli powder

To Cook

1 Heat the oil in a large saucepan, add the chicken and fry for 5–10 minutes, turning frequently, until well browned.

2 Lift out the chicken pieces and put them in a large dish. Mix **BOWL 1** thoroughly and coat the chicken all over with the mixture. Cover and set aside to marinate for 5–10 minutes.

3 Add the onions to the oil in the pan and fry for 5–10 minutes until golden brown and starting to caramelise.

4 Add the chicken, along with the vindaloo marinade, to the pan and cook over a medium to low heat for 10 minutes, stirring occasionally.

5 Pour in the stock and simmer for 5 minutes, stirring from time to time.

6 Add **BOWL 2**, stir well and cook for another 5 minutes.

7 If you want a really hot dish, add **BOWL 3**, stir well and bring to the boil.

8 Reduce the heat and simmer gently for 20–30 minutes, stirring occasionally, until the chicken is tender and falls away from the bone.

COOK'S TIPS If you want to reduce the fieriness, remove the seeds from the chillies to keep the taste but reduce the heat, or leave them out altogether. Remember to wash your hands after cutting or de-seeding chillies. If there are bits of fried chicken left on the base of the pan, this is a good thing and will make the sauce tastier. Only add bowl 3 if you want to make the dish really hot. I think this is unnecessary because the spices already added up to this point make a very spicy and tasty dish. However, if you really like to sweat (quite a lot!), add bowl 3 at your peril.

Chicken Tikka Masala
This is a truly Anglo/Indian dish, made by Indian people for the British because of their love of sauces and mild flavours. This is a simplified version of the dish, although it is still a bit fiddly to cook because it is really two recipes combined into one.

PREPARATION: 15 mins
COOKING: 30–40 mins
SERVES: 4–6 people

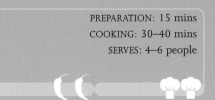

MURGH TIKKA MASALA

Ingredients

4 tablespoons sunflower oil
chicken tikka plus reserved marinade (page 23)
300ml/½ pint single cream
juice of ½ lemon
handful coriander, coarsely chopped

BOWL 1
1 large onion, finely chopped
2 red peppers, de-seeded and chopped

BOWL 2
2 teaspoons garam masala
2 teaspoons paprika
2 teaspoons ground coriander
¼ teaspoon ground cardamom

BOWL 3
2 cloves garlic, crushed
2.5cm/1in piece fresh ginger, peeled and grated or finely chopped
1 teaspoon salt
2 teaspoons sugar
2 tablespoons tomato purée

To Cook

1 Heat the oil in a large pan, add **BOWL 1** and fry for 5–10 minutes until the onion and peppers are browned and slightly caramelised.
2 Add **BOWL 2** to the pan and cook for 2–3 minutes.
3 Add **BOWL 3** and the reserved marinade from the chicken tikka with 300ml/½ pint hot water. Mix well and simmer for 10–15 minutes.
4 Remove from the heat and add the cream. Mix well and return to simmer for 2 minutes.
5 Add the chicken tikka and simmer gently for about 5 minutes.
6 Sprinkle over the lemon juice and stir in the coriander.

COOK'S TIPS You may like to cut the chicken tikka into slightly smaller 2.5cm/1in cubes when using it to make chicken tikka masala. If the onion and pepper mixture gets too dry while cooking, add a little water.
SERVING SUGGESTION Serve with basmati rice and dry hot potato (page 125).

Chicken Biriyani
Biriyanis descend from the rich style of Mongolian cooking. Made for emperors, this dish is a tasty and satisfying meal in itself.

PREPARATION: 30 mins plus
1 hour marinating
COOKING: 50–60 mins
SERVES: 4–6 people

MURGH BIRIYANI

Ingredients

8–12 chicken thighs, skinned
4 tablespoons olive oil
50g/2oz sultanas
2 large onions, finely sliced
450g/1lb long grain rice, washed and soaked in water for 10 minutes and then drained
2 tablespoons butter, melted
pinch of saffron strands, steeped in a little hot water

BOWL 1
1 teaspoon garam masala
1 small onion, finely sliced
2 cloves garlic, crushed
5cm/2in piece fresh ginger, peeled and grated
450ml/³/4 pint natural yoghurt

BOWL 2
50g/2oz almonds, chopped
50g/2oz cashew nuts, chopped

BOWL 3
4 bay leaves
4 cloves
8 black peppercorns
4 green cardamom pods
1 brown cardamom pod, crushed
5cm/2in cinnamon stick
1 teaspoon turmeric

To Cook

1 Mix the chicken with **BOWL 1** and leave to marinate for 1 hour.
2 Heat the oil in a large saucepan and lightly fry **BOWL 2** for 1–2 minutes. Set aside, mixed with the sultanas.
3 Fry the onions in the saucepan until golden brown. Set aside half the onion for garnishing.
4 Add **BOWL 3** to the remaining onion in the pan and cook for another 1–2 minutes.
5 Add the chicken and marinade, mix well and cook for another 20 minutes, stirring occasionally.
6 Add the rice and mix in well.
7 Pour in 900ml/1¹/2 pints warm water and cook gently for another 15 minutes.
8 Add the almond, cashew and sultana mixture and cook for another 5–10 minutes until the water is absorbed and the rice is tender.
9 Pour the melted butter and saffron into the pan and mix well.
10 Adjust the seasoning if necessary and garnish with fried onions.

COOK'S TIP Wash the rice thoroughly. Leave out the nuts, if allergic.
SERVING SUGGESTION This dish is an entire meal. It can be served with salad and red lentils (page 34) or lentils with spinach (page 113)

FISH AND SEAFOOD

4

Sweet and Spicy Fish Curry
This recipe is ideal for lovers of sweet, spicy food who also enjoy fish. The fish is sealed with spice to give it a golden colour and then gently poached in an exotic sweet masala sauce. The result is delicious.

PREPARATION: 15–20 mins
COOKING: 35–40 mins
SERVES: 3–4 people

MUSHALLAR MAS TARKARI

Ingredients

1kg/2lb white fish steaks
4 tablespoons sunflower oil
1 teaspoon sugar
2 teaspoons salt
2 handfuls chopped coriander leaves

BOWL 1
2 teaspoons turmeric
1 teaspoon salt

BOWL 2
1 large onion, thinly sliced
2 cloves garlic, crushed

BOWL 3
2 teaspoons ground cumin
3 bay leaves

BOWL 4
2.5cm/1in piece fresh ginger, peeled and roughly chopped
1 red chilli, trimmed and sliced
1 teaspoon cumin seeds
1 teaspoon coriander seeds

BOWL 5
2 tablespoons natural yoghurt
2 tablespoons clear honey

To Cook

1 Place the fish steaks in a dish, add **BOWL 1** and coat the fish all over.

2 Heat the oil in a large frying pan, add the fish and fry gently for 5 minutes until light golden brown on both sides. Remove from the pan and set aside.

3 Add **BOWL 2** to the pan and fry for 4–5 minutes until the onion is golden brown.

4 Add **BOWL 3**, mix well and fry for 2 minutes.

5 Place **BOWL 4** in a blender with 150ml/¼ pint water and process to a smooth paste. Add to the pan and cook, stirring, for 3 minutes.

6 Reduce the heat, add **BOWL 5** and mix well. Cook for 2–3 minutes to blend the flavours.

7 Add the sugar and salt with 150ml/¼ pint water and bring to the boil. Return the fish to the pan and stir carefully to coat with the sauce, taking care not to break the fish up.

8 Reduce the heat and simmer gently for 10 minutes until the liquid has thickened a little and the fish is cooked. Adjust the seasoning if necessary and stir in the coriander.

COOK'S TIPS When preparing the fish, make sure the steaks are thoroughly covered with the spices. Take care not to overcook the fish or it will turn rubbery. To give the dish extra bite, add 1–2 sliced fresh green chillies when you fry the onion and garlic. **SERVING SUGGESTIONS** Goes well with spinach and potato (page 112) or fried ladies fingers (page 121).

Bream Curry with Coconut Milk

This is a rare dish, not widely known outside Bengal. I have substituted bream for the traditional hilsa mass because it is more widely available.

PREPARATION: 15–20 mins
COOKING: 40–50 mins
SERVES: 2–4 people

NARIKEL MAS TARKARI

Ingredients

450g/1lb bream steaks
1 teaspoon salt
3 tablespoons sunflower oil
1 large onion, finely chopped
2 handfuls chopped coriander leaves

BOWL 1
1 teaspoon turmeric
1 teaspoon chilli powder
1 teaspoon ground coriander
1 teaspoon paprika
$^1/_2$ teaspoon ground ginger

BOWL 2
2 cardamom pods
5cm/2in cinnamon stick
juice of 1 lemon

BOWL 3
4 green chillies, trimmed and sliced lengthways
125ml/4fl oz coconut milk

To Cook

1 Rub the fish all over with salt and set aside.

2 Heat the oil in a large frying pan, add the onion and fry gently for about 5 minutes until soft.

3 Mix **BOWL 1** to a smooth paste with 300ml/$^1/_2$ pint water. Add to the pan and fry for 5–6 minutes until the onion is golden brown.

4 Add another 300ml/$^1/_2$ pint water and bring to the boil. Reduce the heat and add the fish with **BOWL 2**. Mix well, cover and simmer for 10–15 minutes until the sauce becomes thick.

5 Turn the pieces of fish over and mix in **BOWL 3**. Cook for another 10–15 minutes until the oil starts to separate out on the surface.

6 Adjust the seasoning if necessary and stir in the coriander.

COOK'S TIPS You can use mackerel, salmon, haddock, lobster or prawn instead of bream. If the sauce is too thin, lift out the fish while you boil the liquid to reduce it – you don't want to overcook the fish – then return it before serving.
SERVING SUGGESTION Serve with spiced pullao rice (page 46).

Haddock Korma
There are many ways to cook korma but fish korma is not as well known as meat dishes such as chicken or lamb korma. This recipe shows how korma-style cooking can be used to create a delicious fish dish.

MAS KORMA

PREPARATION: 15 mins plus
15 mins marinating
COOKING: 30–40 mins
SERVES: 4–6 people

Ingredients

1kg/2lb haddock steaks
3 tablespoons sunflower oil
1 onion, finely sliced
300ml/½ pint fish stock
2 handfuls chopped coriander leaves

BOWL 1

300ml/½ pint sour cream
6 cardamom pods
7.5cm/3in cinnamon stick

BOWL 2

½ teaspoon turmeric
2 teaspoons ground coriander
2.5cm/1in piece fresh ginger, peeled and grated or finely chopped
2 cloves garlic, crushed

BOWL 3

4 green chillies, trimmed and thinly sliced lengthways
1 tablespoon kewra water
2 teaspoons sugar
juice of ½ lemon

To Cook

1 Place the fish steaks in a dish. Mix **BOWL 1** thoroughly and pour the liquid over the fish. Set aside for 15 minutes to marinate.

2 Heat the oil in a large frying pan, add the onion and fry for 4–5 minutes until soft.

3 Add **BOWL 2** and continue frying for 1–2 minutes until golden brown.

4 Add the fish steaks with the marinade and simmer gently for 3 minutes, making sure the fish is evenly covered with the spice mixture.

5 Pour in the stock so that it just covers the fish. Cover and simmer gently for another 10–15 minutes until the sauce has thickened, turning the fish occasionally.

6 Add **BOWL 3** and mix well, taking care not to break up the fish steaks. Simmer gently for 5–10 minutes until the oil starts to separate out.

7 Stir in the coriander.

COOK'S TIPS Use cod, salmon or bream instead of haddock if you prefer. Fish steaks are better for korma-style cooking than fillets. Take care not to overcook the fish; it should keep its firm, moist texture.

SERVING SUGGESTION Serve with pullao rice (page 46).

Spiced Trout with Onions

I remember being on holiday when my parents went to a trout farm, caught some fish and cooked this dish. We had hired a camper van and the rain had been beating down heavily all day, but the smell from the kitchen was wondrous and the memory of the taste lives with me to this day.

PREPARATION: 10 mins
COOKING: 25–40 mins
SERVES: 2–4 people

MAS BHAJI

Ingredients

2 medium trout, gutted and cleaned
3 tablespoons olive oil
1 large onion, sliced
2 handfuls chopped coriander leaves

BOWL 1
½ teaspoon turmeric
1 teaspoon salt

BOWL 2
½ teaspoon ground cumin
½ teaspoon ground coriander
½ teaspoon freshly ground black pepper

BOWL 3
6 green chillies, trimmed and thinly sliced
juice of 1 lemon

To Cook

1 Place the trout in a dish, add **BOWL 1** and coat the fish all over.

2 Heat the oil in a large frying pan and fry the trout for 1–2 minutes on both sides until the skin is sealed and lightly browned. Remove from the pan and set aside.

3 Add the onion to the pan and fry for about 5 minutes until just tender.

4 Add **BOWL 2** and mix well. Continue frying for 1–3 minutes until the onion is golden brown.

5 Return the trout to the pan and cook gently for 10–15 minutes, turning once.

6 Add **BOWL 3**, stir well and cook gently for 5–10 minutes until the trout is just cooked.

7 Adjust the seasoning if necessary and sprinkle with the coriander.

COOK'S TIPS Trout has a very delicate texture so take care not to overcook it. The meat should be soft and juicy. Cook gently to allow the spices to sink deep within the fish.
SERVING SUGGESTION Goes well with dry hot potato (page 125) and spiced pullao rice (page 46).

Herring Curry with Fresh Chillies

This is a quick dish that's really easy to cook. I've spiced it up a bit for those who like things hot.

PREPARATION: 20 mins
COOKING: 30 mins
SERVES: 4 people

MARICHER MAS TARKARI

Ingredients

450g/1lb herrings, scaled, gutted and trimmed
3 tablespoons sunflower oil
1 large onion, finely chopped
6 green chillies, trimmed and thinly sliced lengthways

BOWL 1
½ teaspoon salt
1 teaspoon turmeric

BOWL 2
1 teaspoon chilli powder
1 teaspoon ground coriander
1 teaspoon paprika

To Cook

1 Stir **BOWL 1** and rub the mixture into the herrings, making sure you cover all the flesh, inside and out. Set aside.

2 Heat the oil in a large frying pan, add the herrings and fry gently for 1 minute on each side to seal. Remove from the pan and set aside.

3 Add the onion to the pan and fry for 4–5 minutes, stirring frequently, until golden brown.

4 Mix **BOWL 2** thoroughly with 150ml/¼ pint water and add to the pan. Fry for 2–3 minutes to cook the spices.

5 Return the herrings to the pan, pour in 300ml/½ pint water and simmer gently for 10 minutes.

6 Add the chillies and simmer for another 10 minutes until the fish is just cooked. Adjust the seasoning if necessary.

COOK'S TIPS You can use mackerel instead of herring but this will make it a much more oily dish.
SERVING SUGGESTIONS Serve with rice or naan bread (page 44) and a vegetable of your choice. You could also serve this dish as a starter instead of the usual kebabs or chicken tikka.

Prawn and Courgette Curry
This is a fish dish from Kerala on the southwest coast of India. Although fish curry is not a common choice, you will enjoy this dish because it is really tasty but not too hot, and the combination of courgettes and prawns is superbly succulent.

PREPARATION: 15–20 mins
COOKING: 30–40 mins
SERVES: 4 people

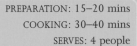

CHINGRI KERALA

Ingredients

4 tablespoons sunflower oil
450g/1lb courgettes, trimmed and cut into 5mm/¼in slices
450g/1lb frozen cooked prawns, defrosted

BOWL 1
1 large onion, thinly sliced
2 cloves garlic, crushed
5cm/2in piece fresh ginger, peeled and grated or finely chopped
1 green chilli, trimmed and thinly sliced

BOWL 2
½ teaspoon chilli powder
½ teaspoon freshly ground black pepper
1 teaspoon turmeric

BOWL 3
1 tablespoon malt vinegar
1 tablespoon clear honey

BOWL 4
2 teaspoons garam masala
2 teaspoons salt

To Cook

1 Heat the oil in a large saucepan, add **BOWL 1** and fry for 5 minutes until the onion is golden brown.
2 Add **BOWL 2** and fry for 2 minutes, stirring continuously to prevent the mixture from sticking.
3 Add the courgettes and **BOWL 3** to the pan and stir to coat the courgettes all over. Cover and simmer gently for 5–10 minutes until the courgettes just begin to soften.
4 Stir in **BOWL 4** with the thawed prawns and cook gently for about 5 minutes until the prawns are heated through. Adjust the seasoning if necessary.

COOK'S TIPS Use tiger prawns for a meatier dish. For a milder taste, omit the green chilli; for a hotter taste, use 2 or 3 green chillies. Avoid overcooking the courgettes by testing them frequently and, if in doubt, undercook them so that they retain their crunchiness.
SERVING SUGGESTION: Serve with boiled basmati rice and vegetables of your choice.

Radish and Prawn Bhaji
This is a simple but delicious recipe. The radish creates an unusual texture with the prawns, making this a juicy and succulent dish to eat.

PREPARATION: 15–20 mins
COOKING: 30–40 mins
SERVES: 4 people

CHINGRI BHAJI

Ingredients

450g/1lb frozen cooked prawns, defrosted
3 tablespoons sunflower oil
2 handfuls chopped coriander leaves

BOWL 1

450g/1lb white radish, peeled and shredded
1 medium onion, chopped
$\frac{1}{2}$ teaspoon turmeric
4 green chillies, trimmed and thinly sliced
100g/4oz frozen peas

BOWL 2

1 teaspoon cumin seeds
1 teaspoon aniseeds
1 teaspoon fenugreek seeds
$\frac{1}{2}$ teaspoon mustard seeds
$\frac{1}{2}$ teaspoon black cumin seeds

To Cook

1 Place the prawns in a dish, add **BOWL 1** and mix well.
2 Heat the oil in a large frying pan, add $\frac{1}{2}$ teaspoon of the spice mixture from **BOWL 2** (store the rest in an airtight container to use another time) and mix well.
3 Add the prawn and radish mixture and stir well. Cover and cook gently for 15–20 minutes, stirring occasionally to prevent sticking.
4 When the radish is cooked through, adjust the seasoning if necessary and stir in the coriander.

COOK'S TIPS The spice mixture is a special blend called panchforan. You can buy it readymade from Indian grocers or mix it fresh yourself, as in this recipe. I personally prefer not to use fenugreek and aniseed because I don't like the flavour, but many people do so I have included these spices in the mixture. Panchforan is used in several lentil and vegetable dishes.
SERVING SUGGESTION Serve with spiced pullao rice (page 46) and a korma dish such as haddock korma (page 97).

Lobster Bhaji

This is one of my favourite recipes and was given to me by my mother. As a child I used to hang around the kitchen, nagging her to cook this dish. Lobster was very expensive, so she rarely cooked it, but when she did it was well worth the wait.

PREPARATION: 20–25 mins
COOKING: 15–20 mins
SERVES: 4 people

GOLDA CHINGRI BHAJI

Ingredients

750g/1½lb shelled lobster meat, cut into 2.5cm/1in chunks
3 tablespoons sunflower oil
1 large onion, thinly sliced

BOWL 1
1 teaspoon turmeric
1 teaspoon chilli powder
1 teaspoon ground cumin
1 teaspoon ground coriander
1 teaspoon salt

BOWL 2
4 green chillies, trimmed and thinly sliced lengthways
4 cloves garlic, crushed
½ teaspoon chilli powder
½ teaspoon ground cumin
½ teaspoon ground coriander
½ teaspoon ground white pepper

BOWL 3
4 tomatoes, sliced
2 handfuls chopped coriander leaves

To Cook

1 Place the lobster meat in a dish, mix **BOWL 1** well and use the mixture to coat the lobster pieces all over.
2 Heat 2 tablespoons of the oil in a large frying pan, add the lobster and fry gently for 1 minute, turning the pieces to seal them on all sides. Lift the lobster out of the pan and set aside.
3 Add the remaining oil and the onion and fry for 2–3 minutes until soft and translucent.
4 Add **BOWL 2** and continue to cook for 4–5 minutes until the onion is golden brown.
5 Return the lobster to the pan, mix well to coat with the spice mixture and cook gently for 5 minutes.
6 Stir in **BOWL 3**, heat through, then adjust the seasoning if necessary.

COOK'S TIPS This recipe works well for most types of fish and is a general method for cooking fish bhaji-style. Try monkfish as an alternative to lobster. If the dish gets too dry during cooking, add a little water.
SERVING SUGGESTION Serve with spiced pullao rice (page 46).

Mackerel with Onions

This is a typical Indian recipe for cooking fish with onions. In fact, dopeyaja means two onions. It is relatively simple to cook and you can use it with all sorts of fish.

PREPARATION: 15–20 mins
COOKING: 25–30 mins
SERVES: 4 people

MAS DOPEYAJA

Ingredients

1 teaspoon salt
450g/1lb mackerel fillets
3 tablespoons sunflower oil
2 medium onions, sliced
300ml/½ pint fish stock

BOWL 1

1 teaspoon turmeric
1 teaspoon chilli powder
½ teaspoon ground ginger
½ teaspoon freshly ground black pepper

BOWL 2

2 tomatoes, skinned and chopped
2 tablespoons chopped spring onion tops
2 handfuls chopped coriander leaves

To Cook

1 Rub the salt into the mackerel flesh and set aside.
2 Heat the oil in a large frying pan, add **BOWL 1** and stir fry for 30 seconds to cook the spices.
3 Add the mackerel and onions and cook for 2 minutes, turning once to seal all over.
4 Pour in the fish stock, mix well, then cover and simmer for 15 minutes.
5 Add **BOWL 2** and cook gently for another 5–10 minutes until the mackerel is just cooked. Adjust the seasoning if necessary.

COOK'S TIPS You can cook this recipe using trout, herring, bream, salmon, pollock or even prawns.
SERVING SUGGESTION Serve with basmati rice.

VEGETABLES

5

Mixed Vegetable Curry

Mixed vegetable curry is a common southern Indian dish that can be made with a variety of vegetables and served with many different dishes. This version uses carrots, cauliflower and green beans. The tomato purée mixed with chilli, black pepper and Indian spices makes this a tasty recipe with a big kick – it's hot but delicious.

PREPARATION: 20–25 mins
COOKING: 25–30 mins
SERVES: 4 people

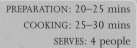

SHABJI TARKARI

Ingredients

1 small cauliflower, trimmed and cut into florets
225g/8oz carrots, peeled and sliced
225g/8oz French beans, trimmed and cut into bite-sized pieces
4 tablespoons sunflower oil
1 large onion, thinly sliced
2 tablespoons tomato purée
450ml/¾ pint chicken or vegetable stock

BOWL 1

½ teaspoon chilli powder
1 teaspoon turmeric
2 teaspoons ground cumin
3 cloves
3 cardamom pods
5cm/2in cinnamon stick

BOWL 2

½ teaspoon freshly ground black pepper
2 teaspoons salt

To Cook

1 Put the cauliflower, carrots and beans in a large saucepan, cover with water and parboil for 3–4 minutes. Drain and set aside.
2 Heat the oil in the same saucepan, add the onion and fry for 3–5 minutes until golden brown.
3 Stir in **BOWL 1** and cook for 2 minutes, stirring continuously.
4 Add the tomato purée, stir well and cook for 1–2 minutes.
5 Add the drained vegetables and stock and stir well. Add **BOWL 2** and simmer gently for 10–15 minutes, stirring occasionally, until the vegetables are completely cooked.

COOK'S TIPS You can use frozen green beans instead of fresh ones, with excellent results. When you drain the vegetables, retain enough of the liquid to use as stock if you're doing a strictly vegetarian version.
SERVING SUGGESTIONS Serve with a meat dish or lentils (pages 34 and 113) and cool it down with a cucumber and tomato salad (page 32), raita (page 38) and some plain boiled rice.

Sweet and Sour Red Cabbage
This southern dish is the Indian equivalent of Chinese sweet and sour, using honey and vinegar to produce the distinctive taste. Such a combination is really delicious when cooked with red cabbage. It will definitely wake up your tastebuds and make you look at cabbages in a new light.

PREPARATION: 10–15 mins
COOKING: 20–25 mins
SERVES: 4 people

LAL BADHAKOPI

Ingredients

3 tablespoons sunflower oil
½ large red cabbage or 1 small red cabbage, finely shredded
1 tablespoon tamarind paste dissolved in 150ml/¼ pint boiling water
1 tablespoon malt vinegar
2 tablespoons clear honey
2 teaspoons salt

BOWL 1
½ teaspoon freshly ground black pepper
1 teaspoon ground coriander
2 teaspoons garam masala

To Cook

1 Heat the oil in a saucepan, add **BOWL 1** and fry for 1 minute, stirring continuously.
2 Add the cabbage and mix well to coat it with the spices, then add the tamarind water, stirring well.
3 Mix in the vinegar and bring to the boil.
4 Add the honey and stir well, then reduce the heat to simmering point.
5 Mix in the salt, cover and simmer gently for 10–15 minutes, stirring occasionally, until the cabbage is cooked as you like it.

COOK'S TIPS Take care not to let the spices burn; only fry them gently for 1 minute or so. Tamarind paste is available from supermarkets and specialist Indian grocers. You could also try this recipe with white cabbage.
SERVING SUGGESTIONS Serve with a meat curry and rice or with a vegetarian dish such as lentils (pages 34 and 113).

Spinach with Potato

Saag aloo originates from the mild climates of northern India where green vegetables and potatoes grow in abundance in the rich, fertile soil. Good-quality meat is more readily available in the north, so vegetable curries tend to be cooked as accompaniments to rich meat dishes, but spinach cooked in this way is a delicious meal in itself.

SAAG ALOO

PREPARATION: 15–20 mins
COOKING: 35–40 mins
SERVES: 4–6 people

Ingredients

750g/1½lb waxy potatoes, cleaned but skins left on
3 tablespoons sunflower oil
1 medium onion, thinly sliced
2 tomatoes, skinned and chopped
450g/1lb frozen spinach, defrosted

BOWL 1

2 cloves garlic, crushed
2.5cm/1in piece fresh ginger, peeled and grated or finely chopped
1 teaspoon turmeric
2 teaspoons cumin seeds
½ teaspoon chilli powder

BOWL 2

1 teaspoon salt
1 teaspoon garam masala

BOWL 3

2 tomatoes, thinly sliced
2 handfuls chopped coriander leaves

To Cook

1 Parboil the potatoes in plenty of water for about 5 minutes. Drain and chop into rough cubes, then set aside.

2 Heat the oil in a large saucepan, add the onion and fry for 5–10 minutes until thoroughly browned or even slightly burned.

3 Add **BOWL 1**, stir well and fry for 2–3 minutes.

4 Stir in the chopped tomatoes and fry for another 2–3 minutes, stirring regularly.

5 Add the potatoes and spinach and mix thoroughly with the spices. Cover and cook gently, stirring occasionally, until the spices have blended in and the potatoes are just tender.

6 Sprinkle with **BOWL 2**, stir carefully and cook for 1–2 minutes to blend the flavours.

7 Add **BOWL 3** and mix thoroughly for a minute or so until the tomatoes are heated through.

COOK'S TIPS If the onion gets too dry when frying, add a little more oil. This recipe uses frozen spinach but you can use fresh if you prefer.
SERVING SUGGESTION This makes a great meal on its own with naan bread (page 44) and pickles.

Lentils with Spinach
Imagine sparkling blue sea lapping against golden sands, ancient temples amid luscious green countryside and a multicoloured atmosphere of music, song and dance. This is the beautiful land of Gujarat on the western coast of India. Palongsak dal is a typical dish from this region and can be served as an accompaniment or as a meal in itself.

PALONGSAK DAL

PREPARATION: 15–20 mins
COOKING: 50–60 mins
SERVES: 3–4 people

Ingredients

225g/8oz red split lentils, well rinsed and drained
225g/8oz frozen spinach, defrosted
2 tablespoons natural yoghurt

BOWL 1
1 medium onion, thinly sliced
1 clove garlic, crushed

BOWL 2
½ teaspoon chilli powder
1 teaspoon ground ginger
1 teaspoon salt

To Cook

1 Place the lentils and **BOWL 1** in a saucepan with 600ml/1 pint water and bring to the boil. Reduce the heat to a simmer.
2 Stir in **BOWL 2**, cover and simmer gently for 30–40 minutes or until the lentils break down and have a soupy consistency.
3 Boil rapidly to evaporate any excess water so that the dal is fairly thick.
4 Add the spinach and stir well. Continue to cook over a moderate heat for 2–3 minutes until heated through and blended.
5 Stir in the yoghurt and simmer gently for 3–4 minutes to heat. Adjust the seasoning if necessary.

COOK'S TIPS When the lentils are cooking, skim off any froth with a large slotted spoon. If the lentils become too dry while cooking, add a little more water. Use 450g/1lb fresh spinach if you prefer; wash well and chop finely.
SERVING SUGGESTIONS Serve with rice or naan bread (page 44) for a satisfying vegetarian meal.

Pea and Potato Curry

This is a staple dish cooked by most people in India and is often served for breakfast with a few chapattis or naan. It is easy to make and can also be used as an accompaniment for a main meal. You will find this dish quite filling.

PREPARATION: 15–20 mins
COOKING: 20–30 mins
SERVES: 4 people

MATARSHUTI ALOO

Ingredients

450g/1lb waxy potatoes, peeled and cut into 2.5cm/1in chunks
2 tablespoons sunflower oil
½ teaspoon salt
450g/1lb frozen peas

BOWL 1

1 medium onion, chopped
2 cloves garlic, crushed
2.5cm/1in piece fresh ginger, peeled and grated or finely chopped
1 tablespoon chopped coriander leaves

BOWL 2

½ teaspoon ground cumin
½ teaspoon chilli powder
1 teaspoon ground coriander
1 teaspoon turmeric

BOWL 3

juice of 1 lemon
1 teaspoon garam masala

To Cook

1 Parboil the potatoes in water for 5 minutes until half cooked. Drain and set aside.

2 Heat the oil in a large saucepan, add **BOWL 1** and fry for 2–3 minutes until the onion is golden brown.

3 Stir in **BOWL 2** and fry for 2 minutes, stirring frequently to prevent the spices from sticking to the pan.

4 Add the potatoes with the salt and stir well to coat the potatoes with the spice mixture.

5 Add the peas, reduce the heat and simmer gently for 5–10 minutes until the vegetables are tender.

6 Add **BOWL 3** and mix well. Cook for another 2–3 minutes. Adjust the seasoning if necessary.

COOK'S TIPS This dry curry makes an excellent mild filling for vegetarian samosas (page 21). Leave out the potatoes altogether to make a pea-only curry if you prefer.
SERVING SUGGESTIONS Serve with rice and a meat curry or with rice and lentils (pages 34 and 113) for a vegetarian meal.

Dry-fried Mushroom Curry
This dish from eastern India tastes absolutely wonderful and requires very little preparation. The thyme and sage create a uniquely Indian/Italian taste that will surprise your palate. It's a taste experience you'll want to repeat.

PREPARATION: 10–15 mins
COOKING: 15–20 mins
SERVES: 4 people

BANGERSATA BHAJI

Ingredients

2 tablespoons sunflower oil
225g/8oz button mushrooms, cleaned and sliced
juice of ½ lemon

BOWL 1
1 small onion, finely chopped
2 cloves garlic, crushed

BOWL 2
½ teaspoon ground cardamom
1 teaspoon dried sage
1 teaspoon dried thyme
½ teaspoon salt

To Cook

1 Heat the oil in a saucepan, add **BOWL 1** and fry for 4–5 minutes until golden brown.
2 Stir in **BOWL 2** with the mushrooms and cook gently for 3–4 minutes.
3 Mix in the lemon juice and cook gently for 2–3 minutes until the mushrooms are tender. Adjust the seasoning if necessary.

SERVING SUGGESTIONS Serve with boiled rice and any meat or vegetable curry of your choice. This dish is also ideal for barbecues as an accompaniment to tandoori chicken bites (page 16) or skewered mince meat (page 20). Although usually served hot, it also tastes good cold with salads.

Spicy Black-eyed Beans
This little-known dish from the Bengal region of India is packed with protein. It has a wonderful texture and a surprisingly hot yet tangy taste that makes for addictive eating.

PREPARATION: 15–20 mins plus
soaking overnight
COOKING: 70–80 mins
SERVES: 4 people

BENGALI SIM

Ingredients

225g/8oz black-eyed beans, soaked overnight in cold water
3 tablespoons olive oil
2 tablespoons tomato purée
juice of 1 lemon
2 tablespoons chopped coriander leaves

BOWL 1
1 large onion, thinly sliced
2 cloves garlic, crushed
2.5cm/1in piece fresh ginger, peeled and grated or finely chopped

BOWL 2
2 dried chillies
½ teaspoon chilli powder
½ teaspoon freshly ground black pepper
1 teaspoon ground cumin
1 teaspoon salt

To Cook

1 Rinse the soaked beans and boil in plenty of fresh water for 45 minutes until tender. Drain and set aside.
2 Heat the oil in a saucepan, add **BOWL 1** and fry for 5 minutes until the onion is golden brown.
3 Add **BOWL 2** and fry for 1–2 minutes, stirring continuously.
4 Mix in the drained beans and tomato purée with 150ml/¼ pint water and cook gently for 10–15 minutes, stirring occasionally.
5 Add the lemon juice and mix well. Stir in the coriander and cook for another 2–3 minutes. Adjust the seasoning if necessary.

COOK'S TIPS If the curry is too dry for your taste, add a little more water with the tomato purée. If you want to give the dish extra bite, add fresh green or red chillies with the dry spices in bowl 2.
SERVING SUGGESTIONS These spicy beans taste great with chapattis (page 42) or naan bread (page 44). You could also serve them as part of a main meal with another vegetable dish and basmati rice.

Carrots with Cashew Nuts

This northern Indian dish is colourful, bright and very easy to make. The cashew nuts give it a special crunchy texture that works well as an accompaniment to Indian meat dishes.

PREPARATION: 15–20 mins
COOKING: 25–30 mins
SERVES: 4 people

GAJJAR BHAJI

Ingredients

3 tablespoons sunflower oil

1 large onion, sliced

450g/1lb carrots, peeled and cut into chunky sticks

300ml/½ pint vegetable stock

225g/8oz cashew nuts

1 teaspoon salt *

2 tomatoes, skinned and coarsely chopped

BOWL 1

5cm/2in piece fresh ginger, peeled and grated or finely chopped

½ teaspoon chilli powder

1 teaspoon garam masala

1 teaspoon plain flour

* omit the salt if using salted cashew nuts

To Cook

1 Heat the oil in a large saucepan, add the onion and fry for 2–3 minutes until softened.

2 Add **BOWL 1** and the carrots and mix well to blend in the flour.

3 Gradually blend in the stock and mix in the cashew nuts (with salt if needed).

4 Cover and simmer gently for 15–20 minutes, stirring occasionally, until the carrots are tender.

5 Mix in the tomatoes and heat through for 2–3 minutes.

COOK'S TIPS Reduce the quantity of cashew nuts by half for a less nutty taste.

SERVING SUGGESTIONS This is a fairly dry curry, particularly well suited as an accompaniment to meat dishes that have a rich sauce, such as red meat curry (page 56) or lamb curry (page 59). Alternatively, serve with lentils (pages 34 and 113) and rice for a satisfying vegetarian meal.

Vegetable Vindaloo
This dish is perfect for vegetarians who like hot food. Vindaloo was originally a Portuguese chicken dish that was adapted by the Goans to give it a bit more bite. This is a vegetarian version of the chicken recipe.

PREPARATION: 15–20 mins plus
2 hours marinating
COOKING: 20–25 mins
SERVES: 4–6 people

SHABJI VINDALOO

Ingredients

3 tablespoons sunflower oil

BOWL 1
350g/12oz potatoes, peeled and diced
100g/4oz peas
2 carrots, peeled and diced
1 onion, thinly sliced
2 green chillies, chopped
2 red chillies, chopped
1 teaspoon chilli powder
1 teaspoon turmeric
1 teaspoon ground cumin
2 cardamom pods
2.5cm/1in cinnamon stick
1/2 teaspoon freshly ground black pepper
1 teaspoon salt
2 tablespoons vinegar

To Cook

1 Mix **BOWL 1** and set aside for 2 hours to marinate.
2 Heat the oil in a large saucepan.
3 Remove the vegetables from the marinade and fry gently for 2–3 minutes until sizzling hot.
4 Add 600ml/1 pint water and any of the leftover marinade, cover and cook for 10–15 minutes until the vegetables are tender.

COOK'S TIPS You can use frozen instead of fresh peas if you wish; they're much more convenient.
SERVING SUGGESTION Vegetable vindaloo is delicious served with paratas (page 43).

Fried Ladies Fingers

Use fresh ladies fingers, or okra, in prime condition. They should be firm to the touch and free from any marks. Test a pod by snapping it in your fingers – it should give a crisp snap.

PREPARATION: 15–20 mins
COOKING: 20–25 mins
SERVES: 4 people

DEROSH BHAJI

Ingredients

3 tablespoons sunflower oil
450g/1lb ladies fingers, cut into 1cm/½in slices
2 tablespoons tomato purée
2 tomatoes, thinly sliced

BOWL 1

1 large onion, finely chopped
2 cloves garlic, crushed

BOWL 2

2 teaspoons ground coriander
1 teaspoon turmeric
½ teaspoon chilli powder
1 teaspoon garam masala

BOWL 3

1 teaspoon salt
½ teaspoon freshly ground black pepper

To Cook

1 Heat the oil in a saucepan, add **BOWL 1** and fry for about 5 minutes until the onion is golden brown.
2 Add **BOWL 2** and cook for 1–2 minutes, stirring gently and making sure the mixture doesn't stick.
3 Add the ladies fingers and **BOWL 3** and cook for 3 minutes, stirring gently to coat with the spices.
4 Add the tomato purée and 3 tablespoons water, mix well, then cover and simmer gently for 5–10 minutes until the okra is cooked.
5 Garnish with sliced tomatoes.

COOK'S TIPS Take care not to crush the ladies fingers when stirring. If the curry is too dry, add a little more water to prevent the ladies fingers from sticking to the pan. When cooked, ladies fingers should be soft but retain a little crunch.
SERVING SUGGESTIONS Serve with basmati rice and main course meat, poultry or fish dishes.

Cabbage and Carrot Curry
Niramish is a technique for cooking vegetables using a special mix of spices. The dish should be kept fairly dry and the spices sparingly used. This is another recipe that makes good eating as a breakfast dish with chapattis.

PREPARATION: 20 mins
COOKING: 20–30 mins
SERVES: 4–6 people

SHABJI NIRAMISH

Ingredients

2 tablespoons sunflower oil
1/2 teaspoon cumin seeds
handful chopped coriander leaves

BOWL 1
1 teaspoon chilli powder
1 teaspoon ground coriander
1 teaspoon salt

BOWL 2
1/2 medium cabbage, coarsely chopped
2 carrots, peeled and diced
100g/4oz peas

BOWL 3
4 tomatoes, skinned and chopped
1 teaspoon sugar

To Cook

1 Heat the oil in a large saucepan, add the cumin and stir fry for 1 minute.
2 Add **BOWL 1** with 150ml/1/4 pint water and fry gently for 3–4 minutes until the water has evaporated.
3 Add **BOWL 2** and stir well to mix with the spices.
4 Cover and cook gently for 15–20 minutes until the vegetables are tender.
5 Add **BOWL 3** and stir well, then heat for 2–3 minutes. Garnish with coriander.

SERVING SUGGESTIONS Serve with chapattis (page 42) or rice.

Roasted Aubergine Curry
This is a lovely curry made by roasting aubergines and then sautéing them with a combination of spices. Buy only fresh aubergines; the ones with a deep purple colour are the best. Beware: the combination of garlic and ginger is fairly strong.

PREPARATION: 30 mins
COOKING: 1 hour
SERVES: 3–4 people

BEGUN BHARTA

Ingredients

2 large aubergines, trimmed and cut into quarters lengthways
2 tablespoons olive oil
2 tomatoes, skinned and chopped
2 tablespoons chopped coriander leaves

BOWL 1
1 onion, coarsely chopped
3 cloves
4cm/1½in piece fresh ginger, peeled
1 teaspoon turmeric

BOWL 2
1 red or green chilli, trimmed and thinly sliced
2 handfuls chopped coriander leaves

BOWL 3
1 teaspoon salt
juice of ½ lemon
4 teaspoons ground coriander
½ teaspoon ground cumin

To Cook

1 Preheat the oven to 190°C/375°F/Gas Mark 5.
2 Place the aubergine quarters on a roasting tray with 4 tablespoons water. Cover with foil and cook for 20–30 minutes until they are tender. Set aside to cool, then chop into 1cm/½in slices.
3 Put **BOWL 1** with 4 tablespoons water into a blender and process to a smooth paste.
4 Heat the oil in a saucepan and fry the paste mixture for 4–6 minutes, stirring continuously, until sizzling.
5 Add **BOWL 2** and simmer for 1–2 minutes.
6 Add the tomatoes and simmer for 8–10 minutes until mushy.
7 Add the aubergines with 2 tablespoons water, then simmer for 12–16 minutes until the aubergines are tender but not disintegrating.
8 Add **BOWL 3** with 2 tablespoons water and simmer for 4–6 minutes to blend the flavours. Adjust the seasoning if necessary and stir in the coriander.

COOK'S TIPS For a milder taste, remove the seeds from the chillies, remembering to wash your hands afterwards. If you don't have a blender, crush the garlic, finely shred or grate the ginger and finely chop the onion in bowl 1, then mix well with the turmeric.
SERVING SUGGESTION Serve with spiced pullao rice (page 46).

Dry Hot Potato

This is a typical vegetarian dish from southern India. Bogar describes a way of cooking that involves quickly frying hot spices and then adding vegetables. This allows the vegetables to remain as fresh as possible while soaking up the maximum flavour from the spices.

PREPARATION: 15–20 mins
COOKING: 30–40 mins
SERVES: 3–4 people

ALOO BOGAR

Ingredients

1kg/2lb red potatoes, peeled and cut into 2.5cm/1in chunks
4 tablespoons sunflower oil

BOWL 1

2 cloves garlic, thinly sliced
1 teaspoon ground cumin
$\frac{1}{2}$ teaspoon mustard seeds
5 bay leaves
2 dried red chillies

BOWL 2

1 teaspoon turmeric
1 teaspoon salt

BOWL 3

2 tomatoes, skinned and chopped
2 handfuls chopped coriander leaves
2 green chillies, trimmed and thinly sliced (optional)

To Cook

1 Boil the potatoes in plenty of water until just beginning to soften but do not overcook. Drain and set aside.

2 Heat the oil in a saucepan until slightly smoking and add **BOWL 1**. Cover and cook for 1 minute until you hear the spices crackle and pop.

3 Add the potatoes and **BOWL 2**, stirring well to coat the potatoes with the spice mixture.

4 Add 150ml/$\frac{1}{4}$ pint warm water and mix well. The water should sizzle and steam from the heat.

5 Cover and allow to steam for 3–4 minutes.

6 Add **BOWL 3** and mix well. Cook for another 2 minutes until the potatoes are soft.

COOK'S TIPS Make sure the oil is really hot when you add the spices from bowl 1. This is an essential part of the bogar way of cooking. Use Desirée potatoes for best results. Make sure they are well coated with spices but do not allow them to burn. Beware of the sizzle and steam when you add the water. Leave out the chillies or use a smaller quantity to reduce the kick. You can also reduce the heat by de-seeding the chillies, remembering to wash your hands afterwards.

SERVING SUGGESTION Serve with basmati rice.

DESSERTS AND DRINKS

6

Kulfi Ice Cream
Kulfi ice cream is a rich, exotic dessert that makes the perfect end to any Indian meal. Almonds, sultanas and coconut combine to create truly oriental nectar – a really sweet treat.

PREPARATION: 5 mins
COOKING: 40 mins plus
2–3 hours freezing
SERVES: 4–6 people

KULFI

Ingredients

600ml/1 pint full-fat milk
handful flaked almonds

BOWL 1
450ml/³/₄ pint double cream
2 tablespoons clear honey

BOWL 2
50g/2oz flaked almonds
50g/2oz sultanas
½ teaspoon almond essence
3 teaspoons desiccated coconut

To Cook

1 Pour the milk into a saucepan and heat until it just boils. Stir gently and continue to boil for 5–10 minutes until the liquid has reduced by about half.

2 Remove from the heat and stir in **BOWL 1**.

3 Simmer gently over a low heat, stirring regularly to reduce the liquid to around 600ml/1 pint.

4 Stir in **BOWL 2**, mix well, then pour into a large freezer container. Allow to cool to room temperature, then place in the freezer.

5 Check the container every 20 minutes or so and, when the mixture is on the point of freezing, use a fork to break up the ice crystals. Return the container to the freezer. Repeat the freezing and breaking up process three or four times.

6 Either keep the ice cream in the large container or press it into 4–6 individual containers, then leave to freeze completely.

7 Transfer from the freezer to the fridge 5–10 minutes before serving. Decorate with a few flaked almonds.

COOK'S TIPS Use a whisk to stir the milk and stop it boiling over, and to stir in the cream. Decorate with pistachios instead of flaked almonds for extra colour and additional flavour, if you prefer.
SERVING SUGGESTIONS Serve with Indian sweets such as fritter whirls in syrup (page 133) or sweet dumplings in syrup (page136).

Sweet Rice
This Muslim dish, which probably descended from the Persians, is eaten at special ceremonies such as religious festivities, weddings and funerals. It is very easy to cook and a light way to round off a heavy meal.

PREPARATION: 5–10 mins plus
4 hours soaking
COOKING: 30–35 mins
SERVES: 4–6 people

Ingredients

125ml/4fl oz sunflower oil

225g/8oz basmati rice, washed, drained, covered in water and left to soak for 4 hours

50g/2oz soft brown sugar

½ teaspoon saffron strands

BOWL 1

6 cloves

6 cardamom pods

7.5cm/3in cinnamon stick

½ teaspoon ground mace

BOWL 2

2 tablespoons clear honey

50g/2oz sultanas

50g/2oz slivered blanched almonds

50g/2oz pistachios

To Cook

1 Heat the oil in a large saucepan, add **BOWL 1** and fry gently for 2–3 minutes.

2 Drain the rice and stir it into the pan, making sure that the rice is covered with the oil mixture.

3 Pour over sufficient boiling water to cover the rice, stir in the sugar and bring back to the boil.

4 Add the saffron, reduce the heat, cover and simmer for 15–20 minutes until the rice is cooked *al dente*.

5 Stir in **BOWL 2** and cook for another 5 minutes.

COOK'S TIPS Replace the nuts with chopped dried fruit, such as apricots, for anyone with a nut allergy.
SERVING SUGGESTION This dish is best served hot.

Pistachio Sweetmeat

Not many people attempt to make sweetmeat because it is so much easier to buy it from Indian shops. However, if you do have the courage to try, you'll find it very satisfying both to make and to eat. The pistachios add a delicious extra crunch.

PREPARATION: 10–15 mins
COOKING: 60–70 mins plus cooling time
SERVES: 4–6 people

BARFI

Ingredients

175g/6oz pistachios chopped
1 tablespoon rice flour
50g/2oz ghee
½ teaspoon almond essence

BOWL 1
1.2 litres/2 pints creamy milk
350g/12oz soft brown sugar

To Cook

1 Pour **BOWL 1** into a saucepan and bring to the boil, stirring continuously until the sugar is totally dissolved.

2 Lower the heat and simmer gently for 20–30 minutes until the milk has reduced and started to thicken.

3 Add the pistachios and mix in well. Sift in the rice flour, stir well and continue to simmer for another 20 minutes.

4 Add the ghee, stir well and cook for another 5 minutes. Stir in the almond essence.

5 Grease a large flat tin and pour the mixture into the tin, spreading it out flat.

6 Allow the mixture to cool and then cut it into pretty shapes.

COOK'S TIPS It is important that you do not let any of the mixture stick to the pan during cooking. Stir continuously to keep the sides and base of the pan clear. You can store the sweetmeat for up to a month sealed in an airtight tin.

Fritter Whirls in Syrup

Jallebi is a traditional Indian sweet that you can find in most bazaars in India. I love watching this recipe being made, especially when the whirls of batter are plunged into sweet fragrant syrup and served fresh.

PREPARATION: 20–30 mins plus
3–4 hours rising time
COOKING: 30–45 mins
SERVES: 4–6 people

JALLEBI

Ingredients

sunflower oil for shallow frying

BOWL 1
½ teaspoon saffron strands, steeped in 150ml/¼ pint boiling water
1 teaspoon dried yeast
2 teaspoons sugar

BOWL 2
175g/6oz plain flour
150ml/¼ pint natural yoghurt

BOWL 3
450g/1lb sugar
4 cloves
4 cardamom pods
5cm/2in cinnamon stick

To Cook

1 Mix **BOWL 1** thoroughly and leave to stand for 10 minutes.
2 Mix **BOWL 2** and leave to stand for 10 minutes.
3 Combine the two bowls and mix to make a smooth batter. Whip with a fork for a few minutes, then set aside for 3–4 hours to allow the yeast to work.
4 Heat 900ml/1½ pints water in a saucepan with **BOWL 3**. Mix well and bring to the boil. Reduce the heat and simmer for 15–20 minutes until the syrup is fairly thick. Set aside.
5 Heat the oil to a depth of about 2.5cm/1in in a deep frying pan.
6 Spoon the batter into a piping bag fitted with a small nozzle and squeeze whirls of batter into the oil, making each whirl about 7cm/3in wide. Fry until golden brown.
7 Remove the whirls from the pan, shake off any excess oil and add to the syrup mixture.

COOK'S TIPS To check if the oil is at the right temperature, drop in a little piece of bread. If the bread sizzles and rises straight to the surface, the oil is ready. Although jallebis are best served fresh, they will keep for up to a week.
SERVING SUGGESTIONS Serve jallebis on their own with tea or coffee, or try them hot with some kulfi ice cream (page 128) or plain vanilla ice cream.

King's Bread Pudding
This rich dessert from the tables of the Mogul kings is a delicious combination of pistachios, almonds, cream and saffron.

PREPARATION: 10–15 mins
COOKING: 30–40 mins
plus cooling time
SERVES: 4–6 people

RAJA TUKRA

Ingredients

175ml/6fl oz sunflower oil
8 medium-thick slices white bread, crusts removed and cut diagonally into triangles
2 teaspoons kewra water

BOWL 1
50g/2oz blanched almonds, chopped
175g/6oz pistachios
175g/6oz sultanas

BOWL 2
150ml/¼ pint milk
300ml/½ pint double cream
225g/8oz soft brown sugar

BOWL 3
1 teaspoon saffron strands, steeped in 150ml/¼ pint boiling water

To Cook

1 Heat the oil in a large frying pan, add **BOWL 1** and fry gently for 1–2 minutes. Remove from the pan and set aside.
2 Add the bread to the pan and fry gently until light brown. Remove from the pan and set aside.
3 Add **BOWL 2** and 300ml/½ pint water to the pan and heat until it comes to the boil. Reduce the heat and simmer gently until the liquid begins to thicken.
4 Stir in **BOWL 3** and cook for another 10 minutes until the liquid turns into a fairly thick syrup.
5 To assemble the pudding, place a layer of bread in a dish, add some almonds, pistachios and sultanas and pour over some of the syrup. Add another layer of bread crossways over the first one with some almonds, pistachios and sultanas and pour over some more syrup.
6 Continue until you have used all the bread, almonds, pistachios, sultanas and syrup.
7 Allow to cool completely, then sprinkle kewra water over the top just before serving.

COOK'S TIPS Chill the pudding before serving, ideally for about 2 hours.

Sweet Dumplings in Syrup
Gulab jamun is a classic Indian sweet. Traditionally it involves boiling milk for several hours until the liquid has almost disappeared, but this recipe uses full-cream dried milk with amazingly good results. The fabulous taste comes from the unusual fusion of condensed milk and cream cheese.

PREPARATION: 10–15 mins
COOKING: 40–50 mins
SERVES: 4–6 people

GULAB JAMUN

Ingredients

450g/1lb sugar
sunflower oil for shallow frying
2 teaspoons kewra water

BOWL 1
100g/4oz cream cheese
100g/4oz full-cream dried milk
50g/2oz self-raising flour
1 tablespoon finely chopped blanched almonds
1 tablespoon finely chopped pistachios
1 tablespoon finely chopped sultanas
125ml/4fl oz full-cream milk, warmed

BOWL 2
4 cloves
4 cardamom pods
2.5cm/1in cinnamon stick

To Cook

1 Mix **BOWL 1** thoroughly and leave to stand for 15 minutes.

2 Mix the sugar with 900ml/1$\frac{1}{2}$ pints water in a large saucepan and bring to the boil, stirring to dissolve the sugar before boiling point is reached.

3 Lower the heat, stir in **BOWL 2** and simmer for 15–20 minutes until the liquid has reduced to a light syrup.

4 Work **BOWL 1** into a dough-like substance. Form the dough into 1cm/$\frac{1}{2}$in diameter balls and set aside.

5 Heat the oil in a large saucepan or deep-fat fryer.

6 Fry the cheesy dough balls a few at a time for 2–3 minutes until they are golden brown. Lift out with a slotted spoon and drain on absorbent paper.

7 Add the fried balls to the syrup. As the balls are cooling, add a few drops of kewra water just before serving.

COOK'S TIPS Put a little piece of bread into the oil to check if it is at the right temperature before frying the dough balls. If the bread sizzles and rises straight to the surface, the oil is ready.
SERVING SUGGESTION Serve freshly cooked dumplings with kulfi ice cream (page 128).

Carrot Pudding
This popular pudding is very easy to make. It uses sweetened grated carrot soaked in cream, which may sound unusual but is definitely worth tasting.

PREPARATION: 10–15 mins
COOKING: 1–1½ hours
SERVES: 4–6 people

GAZORER MISTI

Ingredients

2 tablespoons sunflower oil
450g/1lb carrots, peeled and grated
300ml/½ pint double cream, whipped until it forms soft peaks

BOWL 1
6 cardamom pods, de-seeded
6 cloves
5cm/2in cinnamon stick, broken into small pieces

BOWL 2
900ml/1½ pints milk
225g/8oz soft brown sugar

BOWL 3
100g/4oz chopped blanched almonds
100g/4oz chopped pistachios
100g/4oz sultanas

To Cook

1 Heat the oil in a large saucepan, add **BOWL 1** and fry for 2–3 minutes.
2 Add the grated carrots and mix well. Add **BOWL 2** and bring gradually to the boil, stirring continuously to dissolve the sugar.
3 When the sugar has dissolved, continue to boil for 30 minutes until the milk begins to thicken.
4 Reduce the heat to simmering point, add **BOWL 3** and mix well.
5 Add the cream, mix well and simmer for another 15 minutes.

SERVING SUGGESTION Carrot pudding is best served hot. You can serve it cold, but it's not quite as tasty.

Green Mango Drink This is a refreshing drink to serve on hot summer days and is very easy to make.

PREPARATION: 10 mins
COOKING: 10 mins plus
30 mins chilling
SERVES: 4–6 people

SABUJ AAM SHARBAT

Ingredients

4 firm green mangoes, peeled and stone removed
100g/4oz caster sugar
ice cubes

To Cook

1 Place the mango flesh, sugar and 600ml/1 pint water in a blender and process until smooth.
2 Pour the mixture into a jug and refrigerate for 30 minutes.
3 Put as many ice cubes as you wish into individual serving glasses. Stir the drink well to mix, then pour it over the ice cubes.

COOK'S TIPS You can use other types of fruit to create this drink if you prefer. Add more or less sugar to suit your personal taste.
SERVING SUGGESTIONS This fruity drink is very refreshing on a hot summer's day.

Chilli and Mint Yoghurt Drink

This yoghurt drink is a bit unusual – the combination of yoghurt, chillies and mint with the subtle use of spices gives it an interesting and refreshing taste.

PREPARATION: 5–10 mins
COOKING: 10–15 mins
SERVES: 4–6 people

BORHANI

Ingredients

900ml/1½ pints natural yoghurt

BOWL 1
2 green chillies, trimmed and roughly chopped
2 tablespoons chopped mint leaves
½ teaspoon ground white pepper

BOWL 2
1 teaspoon cumin seeds
1 teaspoon coriander seeds

BOWL 3
1 teaspoon salt
1 teaspoon sugar
½ teaspoon ground mustard

To Cook

1 Place **BOWL 1** in a blender and process until blended to a paste.
2 Add the yoghurt and process again until smoothly mixed.
3 Heat a small frying pan and dry roast **BOWL 2** over a low heat, tossing to turn the seeds, then grind in a spice grinder.
4 Combine the ground spices with **BOWL 3**, add to the blender and process again. Adjust the seasoning if necessary.

COOK'S TIPS You can use a coffee grinder to grind spices; it's a lot easier than doing it by hand.
SERVING SUGGESTION This drink is perfect for dinner parties, especially if there is no alcohol.

Lassi Yoghurt Drink

This drink combines yoghurt with fresh milk and is especially designed to quench the thirst in very hot climates. You can make a sweet lassi or a salted one – it's up to you. The recipe is the same; simply replace the sugar with salt.

PREPARATION: 5 mins
COOKING: 5 mins
SERVES: 4–6 people

DAHI SHARBAT

Ingredients

juice of 1 lemon
3 teaspoons sugar or salt
1 teaspoon kewra water

BOWL 1
300ml/½ pint natural yoghurt
450ml/¾ pint milk
2–3 ice cubes

To Cook

1 Put **BOWL 1** into a liquidiser and blend thoroughly for 1 minute or until the ice is crushed.
2 Add the lemon juice, sugar or salt and kewra water and blend again for another minute.
3 Pour into individual serving glasses.

COOK'S TIPS Use low-fat yoghurt and semi-skimmed milk if you are counting calories.

INDEX

Acknowledgements

This book is dedicated with heartfelt thanks
to my wife (possibly the most beautiful
woman in the world), my mother and father,
my aunt (Nanni) and uncle (Nanna), Judy
and Mike Kent, my close friends and my
parents-in-law; my team – Vicky Thomas,
Martyn Gough, Russ Pedder, Rob Heley and
Ana Sanchez; Richard Bandler, my life mentor,
coach and friend (see www.richardbandler.tv;
www.pureNLP.com) and Paula Bandler – a
very special thanks; my editorial team at
Cassell Illustrated – Anna Cheifetz, Michelle
Pickering, Gabrielle Mander, and Polly Powell;
and lastly to my dear grandmother, grand-
father and my adopted uncle Colonel George
Augustus Brigstocke.